Kids Cook!

FABULOUS FOOD FOR THE WHOLE FAMILY

Sarah Williamson & Zachary Williamson

•

ILLUSTRATED BY LORETTA TREZZO-BRAREN

WILLIAMSON PUBLISHING • CHARLOTTE, VERMONT 05445

Library of Congress Cataloging-in-Publication Data

Williamson, Sarah, 1974-
    Kids cook! : fabulous food for the whole family /
Sarah Williamson and Zachary Williamson.
            p.   cm.
    Includes index.
    Summary: A collection of recipes for breakfasts,
lunches, salads, dinners, snacks, and desserts,
with an emphasis on safety and creativity.

    ISBN 0-913589-61-6 :
    1. Cookery—Juvenile literature.   (1. Cookery.)
    I. Williamson, Zachary, 1977-   . II. Title.
    TX652.5.W554   1992
    641.5'23—dc20   91-38513
                                            CIP
                                            AC

Cover illustration: Loretta Trezzo Braren
Cover and interior design: Trezzo-Braren Studio
Printing: Capital City Press

Williamson Publishing Co.
Box 185
Charlotte, Vermont 05445
(800) 234-8791

Manufactured in the United States of America

10 9 8 7 6 5 4 3 2 1

CONTENTS

dedication

To our grandma, Golde Soloway, for teaching us so much and for being so very special

acknowledgements

We'd like to thank everyone who helped us and encouraged us, and especially everyone who shared their ideas and recipes with us. Our appreciation to Ken Braren and Loretta Trezzo-Braren for their wonderful book design and terrific illustrations. A special thank you to our aunts Jane Soloway, Debby Sobin, Elaine Dratch, and Linda Williamson, and to our grandma, Eleanor Williamson.

▫ A NOTE FROM SARAH & ZACHARY ▫

For years, we have been telling our parents (who are book publishers) that we could write a book. We would sit at the dinner table and discuss books they were working on, and we just knew that we could do it. Finally, they gave us the chance to prove ourselves. One day they came to us with a proposition. They said that they knew we could cook and we claimed that we could write, but could we make it all come together in the form of an exceptional cookbook for kids? Our response was that of course we could. That was the beginning of endless testing, tasting, creating, and many long hours at the computer.

For as long as we remember, we have been going to family picnics, parties, and celebrations of all kinds. To tell you the truth, there were times when we were less than thrilled to be there. The only way to remedy our lack of enthusiasm was to sample every type of food that was being offered. Eventually, we began to find favorite dishes at these gatherings. Before we went home, we would usually ask the host or hostess for a recipe or two. This ritual went on for years, until our recipe box was bursting with recipes for delicious foods.

When our friends and family heard that we were writing a cookbook, they were excited for us. Our Grandmother Golde was so pleased that she told all of her friends about our project, and we began receiving recipes from all over the country. Recipes poured in and soon we had so many that we had trouble choosing the best ones to include in our book. Truthfully, we don't know where many of these recipes originated.

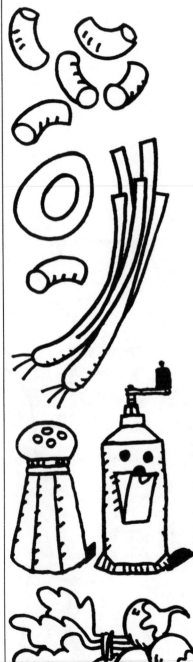

For sure, some are an aspiring chef's brilliant creations, others are old family favorites, and we cooked up others in our kitchen at home.

We are not expert cooks, but we enjoy cooking (and eating). We learned to cook because both of our parents work and oftentimes we helped in the kitchen, getting dinner ready. Soon, we were able to prepare dinner ourselves. One thing we do know for certain — if we can cook, then so can anyone else who wants to. There really is no mystery about it. It just involves reading and following directions.

Our goal was to turn this book into an experience that kids could not get from any other cookbook. Our main criteria was that the recipes had to be for "real" food, not "cute" food that looked like fun, but didn't taste good. And, too, we wanted kids to realize that cooking can be very relaxing and enjoyable. Our book has simplified instructions, so that cooking will be fun instead of frustrating. Cooking is a great way to spend time, either by yourself or with others. In fact, some of the most precious memories we have are of cooking with our Grandmother Golde and our cousins.

So, if you are home from school early and want some "real" food to eat, or if you are responsible for putting dinner on the table one night a week, find a few recipes that tempt you. If you want to lift a cranky parent or overtired sister or brother into a better mood, then bake a batch of cookies and make some tea or hot chocolate. If you like to mix it up in the kitchen and create some culinary masterpieces, or if you babysit a lot and are looking for something fun to do, then leaf through this book and cook up some good food and good fun, too.

Sarah Williamson

Zachary Williamson

Getting started in cooking is really pretty easy. If you can read (or if someone can read directions to you) and you can follow directions (just do one thing at a time), then you can cook. To make sure that there are no areas for confusion, we thought we would go over kitchen safety, the basic kitchen utensils (make substitutions if you don't have the exact tool), and the terms we will be using throughout the book. If you already know most of this, then just read the part on kitchen safety and get cooking!

KITCHEN SAFETY

The kitchen is a fun place to be, and in many families, it is the center of activity. While someone is cooking, someone else may be setting the table, doing his or her homework at the kitchen table, or playing a game. Kitchens are often the most popular room in the house.

It's nice to have lots of company in the kitchen, but it brings up the whole issue of kitchen safety. Let's face it: there are a lot of dangerous things in the kitchen, too. There are stoves with pots filled with hot foods, there are electrical appliances, there are boiling liquids, steam, and hot dishes, and there are sharp knives and utensils. None of these things need to cause a problem as long as you are always careful.

HOUSE RULES

What are the rules in your house about the kitchen? Ask the adult in charge if you are allowed to use the stove when no one is home. Find out if you are allowed to use sharp knives or electrical appliances. If you are not allowed to use these things, then don't. As you get older and get more kitchen experience, you will be able to do more and more by yourself. There are still things we are not allowed to do like deep-fat fry, even after we wrote a whole book about cooking. There are plenty of recipes that you can prepare even if you are not yet allowed to do too much in the kitchen without adult supervision.

Ask if you are allowed to cook with an older brother or sister or with a baby-sitter. Every house has different rules so be sure to check out yours.

SAFETY ALERT!

We scattered a lot of safety tips throughout our book, but some of them are so important we thought we would put them in one place.

Fire Safety

Find out if you have permission to use the stove, toaster, and microwave. If not, don't use them.

Keep emergency numbers by the phone.

Don't cook when wearing shirts with long, baggy sleeves or with your hair hanging down in your face. You could catch on fire.

Use pot holders when handling hot pots, pans, and dishes.

Steam burns. Be careful of escaping steam when lifting casserole or saucepan lids.

Place little children in a playpen when you are working at the stove, so you won't trip over them.

Be very careful of boiling water and other boiling liquids. They can cause very serious burns. WE HAVE MARKED EVERY RECIPE WITH BOILING WATER WITH THIS SYMBOL.

If you are not allowed to handle boiling water alone, plan on getting some help. This is very important.

Never heat a pan full of oil. Use very little oil at a time — like one or two tablespoons at most. It's much safer and much healthier.

Smother a pan fire by covering it with the pan lid. Do not lift a burning pan to try to move it, and DO NOT POUR WATER OVER IT.

Appliance Safety

Only use appliances you have permission to use.

Never submerge an electrical appliance in water. If one accidentally lands in the water, never reach in to remove it.

Never use appliances near the sink or other water sources. Ask your parents to consider having safety outlets installed near sinks in the kitchen and bathrooms.

To clean an appliance like an electric mixer, unplug it and remove the beaters and wash them. Wipe the mixer itself with a damp sponge or cloth, but don't wash.

Knife Safety

Find out if you are allowed to use sharp knives. If not, don't.

Always use an appropriately sized knife. Usually a paring knife or a small slicing knife will fill most of your cooking needs. Never use a knife that is too big for the job you want to do.

Pay attention to what you are doing. Don't try to use a knife while giving directions to other people around you. Look at what you are doing.

Never use a dull knife, as this is more dangerous than using a sharp knife correctly.

Keep knives away from the edges of counters and tables where little ones might grab them.

When you walk with a sharp knife, keep the sharp end pointed down.

USEFUL UTENSILS

Here are some of the most useful utensils for cooking. You may not have the exact same things, so improvise. Make sure that you use a saucepan or bowl that is big enough. The saucepan should always have plenty of extra room so liquids won't boil over the sides. The bowls should be big enough to combine lots of different ingredients. You don't really need to have any electrical appliances to do most of these recipes, although a hand-held electric mixer sure comes in handy. A blender or food processor is needed for a very few recipes, but you can skip those if necessary.

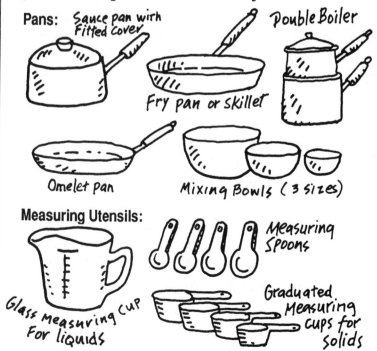

Pans: Sauce pan with Fitted Cover — Double Boiler — Fry pan or skillet — Omelet pan — Mixing Bowls (3 sizes)

Measuring Utensils: Glass measuring cup for liquids — Measuring Spoons — Graduated Measuring cups for solids

Utentils: Rubber Spatula — Wooden Spoons — Paring Knife — Electric Mixer (hand held) — Metal Spatula — Sifter — Metal Grater — Wire Whisk

Baking Pans and Dishes: Casserole Dish with Cover — Cookie Sheet — Muffin Pan — Wire Rack for Cooling — 9"x 9" Baking Pan — 9"x 13" Baking Pan — Layer Cake Pans — Bundt Cake Pan — Loaf Pan for Breads — Pie Dish

WHAT'S THE DIFFERENCE?

Although many cooking terms seem closely related, there are slightly different techniques that do make a difference in how something you are cooking turns out. For example, when you saute something, you cook it in very little oil until it is lightly browned; when you fry something, it is often cooked in more oil or shortening, until it is deeply browned. The taste is very different. Here are some similar terms compared with each other.

MIXING IT ALL UP!

Beat. When you mix rapidly, smoothing out batter and adding air by lifting batter up and over with each stroke. You can use an electric mixer, a wooden spoon, or a wire whisk to beat batter.

Combine. To combine ingredients, either mix or toss so that the ingredients are evenly distributed. Use a wooden spoon (or two spoons to toss).

Cream. Mix with a wooden spoon pressing ingredients against the side of the bowl until the mixture turns creamy. Usually you will be "creaming" together margarine and sugar.

Fold. When you fold in an ingredient, you are trying to distribute a light ingredient like whipped cream throughout a heavier batter without losing the fluffiness. To do this, you very gently turn the ingredients over from the bottom to the top, but do not stir. Use a wooden spoon.

Mix. When you mix ingredients together, you are often combining together dry ingredients like flour and sugar, creamy ingredients like margarine creamed with sugar, and liquid ingredients like water or milk. The goal is to have everything distributed evenly so there are no clumps of just one ingredient. Use a wooden spoon.

Stir. Stirring is what you do when you mix liquids or melted ingredients. Often you stir to keep things from burning on the stove. Use a large spoon.

Whip. To whip, you need to beat the ingredients very rapidly with a wire whisk or an electric mixer. Your goal is to add air to the ingredients so they are very fluffy and sometimes form peaks like whipped cream or egg whites.

Whisk. To whisk is to beat ingredients together until they are well blended and smooth, but not as fluffy as when you whip them. Use a wire whisk or a fork to do this.

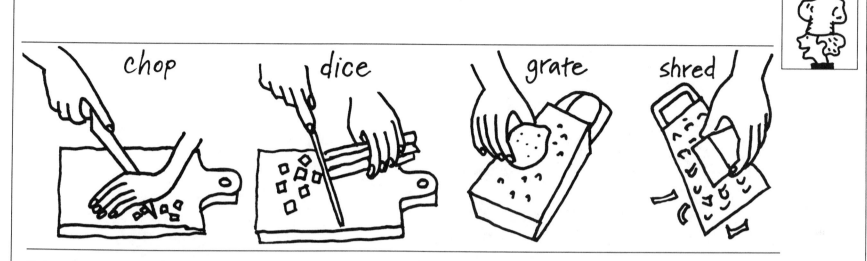

chop   dice   grate   shred

CUTTING UP IN THE KITCHEN

Chop. To chop ingredients is to cut something into small, but not mushy, pieces. To do this you can use a food processor, a blender, or a wooden bowl with a food chopper (these can be very sharp so get adult help). If you aren't allowed to use these appliances and utensils, then just cut the ingredients into small pieces with a knife.

Cut. When cutting, you are breaking something into small pieces. Sometimes they will be cut into matchstick-sized pieces called "julienne," or chunks, or thick slices.

Dice. Dicing is cutting something into tiny square pieces, like little pieces of ham or cheese in a chef salad. This is usually done with a sharp knife. It's almost like chopping, except the pieces are a little neater and sometimes smaller.

Grate. When you rub a solid food, like cheese or a potato, against a metal grater, you get thin shreds of cheese or potato. Some metal graters have different sizes for the openings, so you can get very fine pieces, or thicker shreds.

Mince. When you mince, you chop into very fine particles, such as mincing garlic. This can be done with a garlic mincer.

Puree. When you puree something, you actually take solids such as tomatoes or cooked potatoes, and you blend them so well in a food processor, blender, or food mill that they turn into a heavy liquid-like consistency. This is done with a lot of creamed soups.

Shred. When you cut or grate something like cheese into thin, uneven strips, you are shredding. Usually you use a metal grater to do this.

Slice. When you cut into thick pieces or strips, you are slicing. Using a sharp knife is actually safer than using a dull knife, if you handle the knife correctly (see Kitchen Safety).

Boil   Fry   Stir-Fry

STOVE-TOP COOKING

Boil. When something is boiling, bubbles are rising rapidly to the surface. Because boiling ingredients are very hot, please be careful around them. Use a saucepan that is large enough to prevent ingredients from boiling over onto the stove.

Brown. When you cook in a small amount of oil in order to give food some color, it is called "browning." The goal of browning is usually not to cook completely through.

Fry. To cook in a fry pan or skillet with quite a lot of oil or shortening, until the food is heavily browned and cooked completely through.

Saute. To cook quickly and lightly in as little oil as possible in a fry pan or skillet. Oftentimes, you saute thin slices of chicken, fish, meat, or sliced vegetables to soften them.

Simmer. When you cook something that is just below the boiling point on top of the stove so that bubbles rise very slowly to the top, you are simmering it. Oftentimes, soups are simmered so that the flavors blend slowly together, as the ingredients cook.

Stir-fry. If frying is the heaviest and greasiest, than stir-frying is the lightest, with sauteing in the middle. To stir-fry, you quickly cook vegetables or thinly sliced meat in a hot skillet or wok (if you have one) with a very tiny amount of oil. The goal is to cook so quickly and stir constantly so that foods like vegetables keep their bright colors, crispness, and shape.

MEASURING UP

Knowing how to use measures and change from tablespoons to cups, or from U.S. measures to the metric measures used in Canada can be very helpful when cooking. Here are some handy measures and conversion tables to help you.

Equivalent yields

1 lemon = 3 tablespoons lemon juice
4 ounces firm cheese (cheddar or Swiss) = 1 cup shredded cheese
3 ounces hard cheese (Parmesan) = $\frac{1}{2}$ cup grated cheese
$\frac{1}{4}$ pound (1 stick) butter or margarine = $\frac{1}{2}$ cup = 8 tablespoons
1 square baking chocolate (semi-sweet or unsweetened) = 1 ounce
4 ounces almonds or walnut meats = 1 cup chopped nuts

Metric conversion table

TO CHANGE	TO	MULTIPLY BY
ounces (oz.)	grams (g)	28
pounds (lbs.)	kilograms (kg)	0.45
teaspoons	milliliters (ml)	5
tablespoons	milliliters (ml)	15
fluid ounces (fl. oz)	milliliters (ml)	30
cups	liters (l)	0.24
pints (pt.)	liters (l)	0.47
quarts (qt.)	liters (l)	0.95
gallons (gal.)	liters (l)	3.8
Fahrenheit temp. (°F)	Celsius temp. (°C)	5/9 after subtracting 32

Weights & measures

LIQUID MEASURE EQUIVALENTS
3 teaspoons = 1 tablespoon
2 tablespoons = 1 fluid ounce
4 tablespoons = $\frac{1}{4}$ cup
5 tablespoons + 1 teaspoon = $\frac{1}{3}$ cup
8 tablespoons = $\frac{1}{2}$ cup = 4 fluid ounces
2 cups = 16 fluid ounces = 1 pint
4 cups = 2 pints = 1 quart
1 quart = .946 liters (946.3 milliliters)
1 liter = 1.06 quarts
4 quarts = 1 gallon

DRY MEASURE EQUIVALENTS
2 pints = 1 quart

WEIGHT OR AVOIRDUPOIS EQUIVALENTS
16 ounces = 1 pound
2.2 pounds = 1 kilo

HEALTHY CHOICES

There are lots of choices you can make to eat healthier foods. We've put in Nutri Notes throughout the book, because we know that most kids want to take care of themselves. Here are a few of the healthy choices we use often:

Cook with canola oil or safflower oil.

Substitute plain non-fat yogurt for sour cream.

Never use solid shortenings or lard.
If we can't substitute canola oil, we use margarine.

Use low-fat cheeses, and mozzarella made with part-skim milk.

Use 1 percent milk or skim milk.

Omit the salt or put in half the salt the recipe calls for.

Omit mayonnaise or margarine on sandwiches
and use mustard instead.

Eat whole wheat bread.

Eat fresh fruit and vegetables every day.

Eat breakfast every day.

Try to eat a balanced diet every day.

Get some exercise every day.

Snack on something nutritious before having a sweet treat.
(That way you eat fewer sweets.)

EASY, EASIER, EASIEST!

We remember very clearly what it was like when we learned to cook. We would look at a recipe and if it had too many ingredients, we would skip it. Then we learned that, actually, some of the easiest recipes, like salads, have a lot of ingredients, but there is very little cooking involved — just a lot of combining. So now we know that the number of ingredients has little to do with how difficult a recipe is to prepare.

Some recipes definitely involve more cooking techniques than others. We have marked the recipes with measuring spoons so that you can tell the easiest from those that are just a little bit more involved. All of the recipes are fairly easy, but if you are just beginning to cook you may want to select from the recipes marked with one measuring spoon. Remember the idea is to have fun and end up with some good food, so choose recipes you are comfortable preparing.

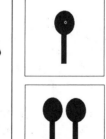

One measuring spoon = Easiest

Two measuring spoons = Slightly more challenging, but you can do it!

Three measuring spoons = A little more involved; if you are just beginning to cook, you might want an experienced cook around the first time you try it.

DISHES, DISHES, & MORE DISHES

Cooking is great fun, and eating is even better, but do you know anyone who loves doing the dishes? We don't, although there are times when it doesn't seem so bad.

This is the approach we take to dishes . . . . someone has to do them, and it better not be Mom or Dad when they get home from work. Usually, our rule is whoever cooks doesn't have to clean up. Sometimes, though, no one else is home. Then we usually turn up the radio, get organized, and get washing. It's not so bad after all. And, as our mom always says to us, "Don't forget to wipe off the counters, too."

Weekday breakfasts in our house are fairly routine, although when we get tired of the usual cereal, fruit, English muffins or bagels, and juice, someone will get ambitious and prepare a fresh fruit salad or bake some muffins the night before — maybe even a coffee cake. What a treat it is to have something special on a school morning!

But to be honest, even though we eat breakfast every day, we look forward to breakfast on weekends the most. One of us usually treats the family to something special like *Zach's Famous Omelet, Dad's Belgian Waffles*, or one of Sarah's special coffee cakes. Some freshly squeezed orange juice and hot cocoa with swirls of whipped cream make these breakfasts a great way to start a new day.

The secret to breakfast (since most everything needs to be served hot) is to have some willing helpers in the kitchen. In our house, someone prepares the main dish, while everyone else sets the table, squeezes the O.J., or puts the butter, jam, and syrup on the table. When we have friends over, they pitch in and help just like part of the family. This way we all get to eat together.

BREAKFAST SUNDAE

This is so good that you'll think you're having dessert instead of breakfast, and it's good for you, too.

HERE'S WHAT YOU NEED:

1 small container of non-fat yogurt, vanilla, plain, or your choice

3 kinds of fresh fruit such as strawberries, blueberries, peaches, bananas, grapes, or apples

Granola or Grape Nuts™

Handful of raisins

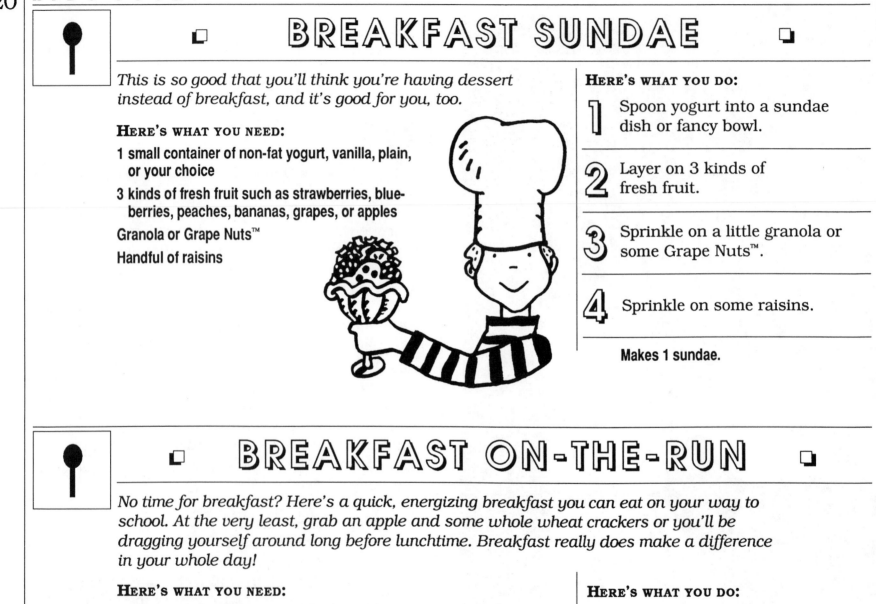

HERE'S WHAT YOU DO:

1 Spoon yogurt into a sundae dish or fancy bowl.

2 Layer on 3 kinds of fresh fruit.

3 Sprinkle on a little granola or some Grape Nuts™.

4 Sprinkle on some raisins.

Makes 1 sundae.

BREAKFAST ON-THE-RUN

No time for breakfast? Here's a quick, energizing breakfast you can eat on your way to school. At the very least, grab an apple and some whole wheat crackers or you'll be dragging yourself around long before lunchtime. Breakfast really does make a difference in your whole day!

HERE'S WHAT YOU NEED:

1 apple (spread with peanut butter if you have time)

4 whole wheat crackers

1 slice of cheese (cheddar, Colby, or whatever you like)

HERE'S WHAT YOU DO:

1 Grab apples, crackers, and cheese, and rush out the door!

Makes enough for 1 person.

BAGEL BROIL

There are all sorts of ways to dress bagels up and down, but here is one of our favorites for days when breakfast just seems too boring. Don't skip over this without trying it, because it tastes better than it sounds.

HERE'S WHAT YOU NEED:

- 1 bagel, split (preferably a raisin bagel, but any kind will do)
- 1 teaspoon margarine
- ½ apple, sliced
- 2 slices of cheddar cheese

HERE'S WHAT YOU DO:

1 Lightly toast bagel. Spread with margarine while still hot.

2 Top each half bagel with sliced apples. Layer cheese on top.

3 Place under broiler (or in toaster oven, use "top brown" feature), until cheese is bubbling. Eat while still hot.

Makes 2 half bagels.

SAFETY ALERT!

If you need emergency help, call 911 if it is available where you live. Otherwise, call the emergency (rescue squad, medical, or fire department) numbers in your area. Make sure you have these numbers at your house and at any house where you baby-sit.

❑ VEGETARIAN ENGLISH MUFFINS ❑

This takes no more than five minutes to put together, and it is a welcome change from the usual breakfast fare.

CLASSY COOKS

Fork-split muffins. What's the big deal about "fork-split" English muffins? Well, one of the best things about English muffins is the nooks and crannies that melted butter and jam can seep into. When you use a fork instead of a knife to split an English muffin, you create these tiny little holes that act as miniature reservoirs. If you split the muffin with a knife, you get a flat surface, and the butter just runs off onto your hands and plate.

HERE'S WHAT YOU NEED:

- 1 English muffin, fork-split
- 1 tablespoon margarine
- 1/2 cup chopped onions, peppers, mushrooms, or other vegetables
- 2 slices of your favorite cheese

HERE'S WHAT YOU DO:

1. Toast English muffin.

2. While muffin is toasting, saute 1/2 cup of mixed vegetables in 1 tablespoon margarine until crisp tender (not soggy).

3. Spoon sauteed vegetables onto muffin halves. Top with slices of cheese.

4. Place under broiler, or use "top brown" feature of toaster oven until cheese is bubbling. Eat while hot.

Makes 2 half English muffins.

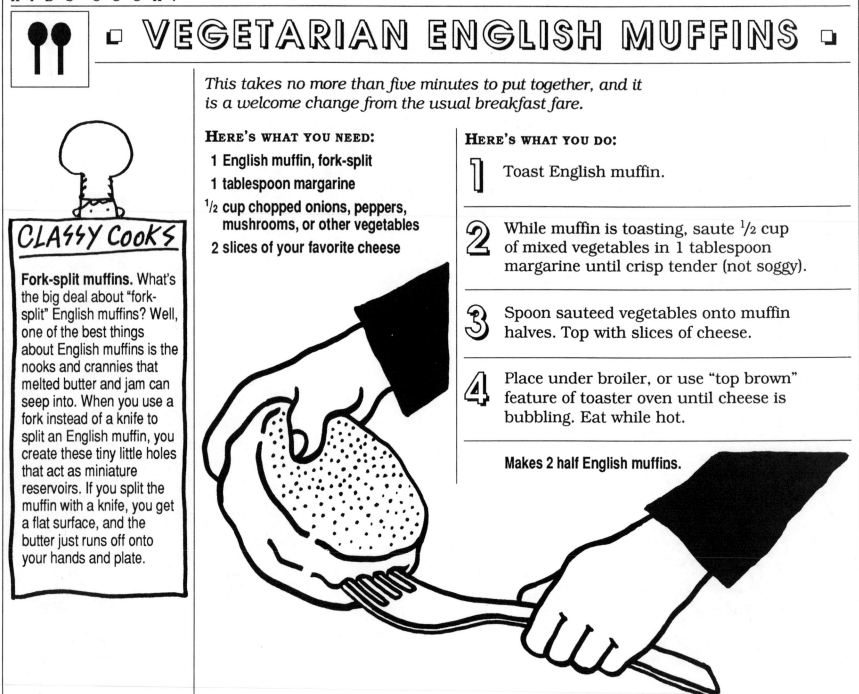

YOUR FAVORITE CEREAL WITH A TWIST

Fresh fruit can make packaged cereal seem like something special. To keep from getting bored with cereal, add whatever fruit is in season.

HERE'S WHAT YOU NEED:

Your favorite cereal

Assorted fruits such as:

½ **apple, sliced**

½ **banana, sliced**

½ **peach, sliced**

¼ **cup blueberries, washed**

¼ **cup strawberries, washed**

¼ **cup raisins**

Milk

¼ **cup nuts, chopped, your choice**

HERE'S WHAT YOU DO:

1 Decide which of these fruits you want on your cereal, and how much of each you would like.

2 Prepare them (make sure they are dried and drained), and put on top of your cereal. Sprinkle with chopped nuts. Top with milk.

Makes 1 bowl of cereal.

NUTRI·NOTE

The four food groups are: milk, meat, fruits and vegetables, and grain. Kids need daily: 3 servings from the milk group, 2 from the meat group, 4 from the fruit and vegetable group, and 4 from the grain group.

MILK

MEAT

FRUIT & VEGGIES

GRAINS

CINNAMON TOAST

This is a favorite treat when we aren't feeling our greatest. A cup of herbal tea with honey, and some cinnamon toast almost makes us feel 100 percent healthy again!

HERE'S WHAT YOU NEED:

3 tablespoons sugar

1 teaspoon cinnamon

$1/2$ **stick margarine, softened**

4 slices bread

Note: You can make the cinnamon-sugar mixture ahead of time, and keep it in an extra salt shaker to sprinkle on your toast in the morning.

HERE'S WHAT YOU DO:

1 Combine sugar and cinnamon in a bowl. Mix well.

2 Toast the bread in the toaster until golden brown.

3 Put the margarine on right away, while toast is still hot.

4 Sprinkle with the cinnamon-sugar mixture.

Makes 4 slices of toast.

HOT CHOCOLATE

Many grown-up cookbooks have complicated recipes for hot chocolate. Frankly, we think the best way to make hot chocolate is to follow the directions on a prepared mix and then add extras to create a special hot drink for yourself!

HERE'S WHAT YOU NEED:

Prepared hot chocolate mix

1 cup milk

Homemade Whipped Cream **(for recipe, see page 97)**

1 stick cinnamon or dash of ground cinnamon (optional)

Options: We are also big fans of topping off our hot chocolate with marshmallow fluff. Of course, some people prefer to float mini-marshmallows in their hot chocolate. The choice is yours.

HERE'S WHAT YOU DO:

1 Heat milk in a saucepan or in the microwave.

2 Pour into a cup and add the hot cocoa mix according to package directions.

3 Swirl on heaps of *Homemade Whipped Cream*. Add a cinnamon stick or sprinkle ground cinnamon on just before serving to make the hot chocolate extra fancy and give it a pleasant aroma.

Makes 1 cup.

ONE-EYED PIRATES

This easy-to-make breakfast will add pizazz to ordinary eggs and toast!

HERE'S WHAT YOU NEED:

1½ tablespoons margarine

2 slices bread, your choice, with a 2" hole cut out of each center

2 eggs

½ jar (8 ounces) spaghetti sauce

2 thick slices of cheese, mozzarella or provolone

HERE'S WHAT YOU DO:

1. Melt margarine in a large skillet on medium heat, and add the bread slices. Brown the bread for 2 to 3 minutes.

2. Crack the eggs and drop into the centers of the bread slices. Cook for one minute, then flip the bread and egg to brown other side.

3. Pour the spaghetti sauce over the bread and continue to cook until egg is cooked to desired doneness.

4. Place cheese slices on top of bread and cover skillet. Turn off heat, and let cheese melt. Serve hot with bacon.

Makes enough for 2 people.

KIDS CAN!

Ashrita Furman did 7400 somersaults in a row. When she was finished, she had rolled over twelve miles!

ZACH'S FAMOUS OMELET

Zach first got into omelet-making when our Uncle Mitch would visit and concoct great omelets. At first Zach helped him, but then they started a friendly competition to see whose omelets were best. Needless to say, no one will judge because we all like eating the entries too much!

HERE'S WHAT YOU NEED:

4 eggs

¹/₄ cup milk

2 tablespoons margarine

Filling:

¹/₂ cup deli ham, diced

¹/₃ cup green or red pepper, washed and diced

¹/₄ cup mushrooms, washed and diced

¹/₄ cup onion, peeled and diced

¹/₃ cup cheese, any kind

1 tablespoon margarine

Dash of pepper

Note: Use your imagination to decide what to put in the filling, but keep the total amount close to about 1²/₃ cups. Also try some herbs. Zach uses basil, oregano, chives, or whatever he can find in the cupboard, garden, or refrigerator. And, of course, you can make great vegetarian omelets, too.

HERE'S WHAT YOU DO:

1 Beat the eggs and the milk together. Set aside.

2 To prepare filling, saute all of the vegetables in 1 tablespoon margarine on medium-high heat.

3 Pour the egg mixture into a well-greased omelet pan, being sure to grease both sides if you are using the "fold-over" style pan.

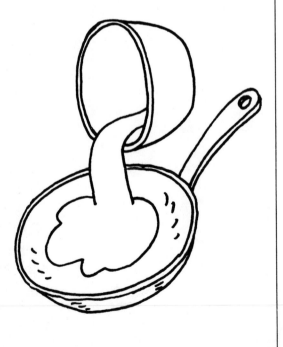

4 Cook on medium heat.

5 When bubbles begin to rise to the top, pour all of the sauteed vegetables onto one side of the pan. Next, layer all of the cheese over the vegetables.

6 When this is done, flip one side of the pan shut, if you have a "fold-over" style pan. If you have an open-faced style pan, gently fold one side of the omelet over the layered side, using a spatula. Cook for about 5 more minutes.

7 When the egg is golden brown, remove from the heat.

8 Flip onto a serving dish by placing a plate over the pan. (The plate should be up-side down.)

9 Carefully, flip the plate and the pan over so that the plate is right side up. (You might want a little help with this; it gets easier with practice.)

10 Lift the pan, and you should have a perfect omelet sitting on the plate.

11 Serve while still warm and enjoy!

Makes enough for 2 to 4 people.

SCRAMBLED EGGS WITH CHEESE

What could be simpler? This is quick enough for a school day when you wake up extra hungry. For a change, why not have a side dish of fresh orange quarters and a cup of hot cocoa!

HERE'S WHAT YOU NEED:

4 eggs

1/3 cup milk

1/3 cup cheese, your choice, shredded or diced

Salt and pepper to taste

Margarine

Options: You can add all sorts of things to scrambled eggs. Try adding several kinds of cheese, chives, sauteed onions, peppers, or mushrooms. Add any or all of these to egg mixture before cooking, but be sure your added ingredients are not soggy and that you don't add extra liquid.

HERE'S WHAT YOU DO:

1. Beat together the eggs and the milk.

2. Mix in the cheese. Add salt and pepper to taste.

3. Melt a pat of margarine in skillet and add egg mixture. Cook on medium heat for 5 to 10 minutes, or until the eggs aren't runny.

Makes 2 servings

EGGS ON TOAST

This is a favorite mid-week treat when we get tired of cereal and fruit. Our dad always used to make this for us when we got up feeling tired. It's easy enough to make for yourself, and with a glass of orange juice it makes a great breakfast.

HERE'S WHAT YOU NEED:

1 egg

1 piece of toast

1 pat of margarine

Salt and pepper to taste

Makes enough for 1 person.

HERE'S WHAT YOU DO:

1. To soft-boil the egg, place in a saucepan with cold water covering the egg. Add about 1/4 teaspoon of salt. Bring water to a simmer (bubbles rising slowly to the surface) over high heat.

2. Once water is simmering, turn heat down and continue to simmer gently for 4 to 5 minutes. Meanwhile, prepare your toast and butter it.

3. Remove the egg from heat and carefully drain. Run under cold water until you can hold egg. With the blunt end of a knife, crack egg open and scoop the insides on top of your buttered toast. Season with salt and pepper and eat right away while it's still hot.

BLUEBERRY PANCAKES

This is one of our all-time favorite breakfasts. You can top these with a pat of margarine, some warm maple syrup, or try some confectioners' sugar. Whatever you choose, be sure to eat them while they're still piping hot!

HERE'S WHAT YOU NEED:

- 1 egg
- 1 cup buttermilk
- 2 tablespoons oil
- 1 cup flour
- 1 tablespoon sugar
- 1 teaspoon baking powder
- ½ teaspoon baking soda
- ½ teaspoon salt
- ½ cup blueberries (fresh are best, but canned or frozen are fine, too.)
- 2 to 3 tablespoons margarine

HERE'S WHAT YOU DO:

1. Blend the egg, buttermilk, and oil together in a bowl.

2. Add all of the dry ingredients (flour, sugar, baking powder, baking soda, salt) to the mixture. Stir until well blended, but it's okay if batter is a little lumpy.

3. Fold in the blueberries.

4. Melt 2 to 3 tablespoons margarine in the pan or on the griddle. Let the griddle get hot so margarine bubbles, but not so hot that it turns brown or smokes.

5. Place spoonfuls of the batter on the griddle. Smaller pancakes are easier to flip.

6. Cook evenly. When bubbles start to appear on the top, and the bottoms are slightly browned, flip the pancakes with a spatula.

Makes about 10 pancakes.

CLASSY COOKS

Pleasing Pancakes. The secret to making pancakes is getting the griddle hot enough. Be sure that the griddle or skillet is hot enough for the margarine to bubble; otherwise the batter will run all over the pan. (Of course, the challenge is not to have it so hot that the margarine turns brown or starts to smoke.) Then, add your batter. You'll get the hang of it after a few tries, so don't get too discouraged if they don't turn out quite right the first few times!

FRENCH TOAST

This is another weekend favorite in our house. French toast is really easy to make, and you can use any kind of bread that you like. Thick slices of French or Italian bread are good. It's delicious served with butter, warm maple syrup, confectioners' sugar, cinnamon sugar, or your favorite marmalade or jam.

HERE'S WHAT YOU NEED:

| 3 eggs | 8 slices bread |
| 1/3 cup milk | Margarine |

HERE'S WHAT YOU DO:

1 Beat the eggs and milk together.

2 Soak each slice of bread for about 2 seconds on each side in the egg mixture.

3 Heat a skillet or griddle to medium high. Melt two tablespoons margarine in the skillet. Add two slices of dipped bread and cook on medium heat, flipping slices occasionally to keep from sticking.

4 Cook until golden brown on each side.

Makes 8 slices.

COTTAGE CHEESE PANCAKES

We admit that these are a little tricky, but once you get the hang of working with the thin batter, you'll be able to make some absolutely light and delicious pancakes. We included them because they are so good. If we can cook them, we know that you can, too!

HERE'S WHAT YOU NEED:

4 eggs

1/2 teaspoon salt

1 tablespoon sugar

1 cup non-fat cottage cheese

1 cup light sour cream

1/2 cup flour

Margarine

HERE'S WHAT YOU DO:

1 In a large bowl, beat all of the ingredients together.

2 Heat a griddle or pan to medium-high with a tablespoon of margarine. Pour a soupspoonful of batter for each pancake onto the hot griddle. You want these to be smaller, "silver dollar"-sized pancakes, so they will be easier to flip. Cook until bubbles start to form on the top, and the top looks solid instead of soupy. Then, using a spatula that has been sprayed with no-stick cooking spray, carefully flip the pancakes.

3 Serve hot with maple syrup and butter, or fresh berries.

Makes enough for 4 to 6 people.

DAD'S BELGIAN WAFFLES

These can be made with a simple waffle recipe on the back of a box of Bisquick™ or use our dad's recipe below. You also can vary the toppings according to your likes.

HERE'S WHAT YOU NEED:

2 eggs

2 cups all-purpose flour (not self-rising)

1³/₄ cups milk

¹/₂ cup vegetable oil

4 teaspoons baking powder

1 tablespoon sugar

¹/₂ teaspoon salt

HERE'S WHAT YOU DO:

1 Spray waffle iron with no-stick spray and then preheat.

2 Beat eggs with mixer. Then add all remaining ingredients and beat until almost smooth.

3 Pour in center of hot waffle iron — about ¹/₂ cup batter at a time. Follow your waffle iron's instructions. Most waffles take about 5 minutes to be cooked through.

4 Transfer to plate, and top with *Fresh Strawberry Topping* (see page 99) and *Homemade Whipped Cream* (see page 97). Serve while very hot.

Makes enough for 4 people.

SAFETY ALERT!

To prevent a kitchen fire, always wear tight fitting sleeves when you cook. Also, don't store things over the stove because you could get burned while reaching for something.

APPLE-CINNAMON MUFFINS

These are great any time of day — after school or for a bedtime snack. When Sarah is in the kitchen banging pots and pans in the evening, we know we're in for a treat the next morning.

CLASSY COOKS

Muffin How-To. Muffins are wonderful, because they are so easy to make and there are so many different kinds. If you have a muffin pan, you can either spray each cup with non-stick cooking spray, grease each cup with shortening, or use paper or foil "cupcake" liners. If you have a recipe that makes fewer muffins, fill the empty cups half full of water so none of the cups are empty. If you don't have a muffin pan, you can use paper liners (double up for added strength) or foil liners. Just place them on a cookie sheet, but check them five minutes earlier to see if they are done.

HERE'S WHAT YOU NEED:

¾ **cup milk**

½ **cup vegetable oil**

1 egg

1 medium-sized apple, peeled, cored, and diced

2 cups flour

⅓ **cup sugar**

3 teaspoons baking powder

1 teaspoon salt

½ **teaspoon cinnamon**

Sugar to sprinkle

HERE'S WHAT YOU DO:

1. Preheat oven to 400°.

2. Beat the milk, oil, and egg together. Mix in the apple chunks.

3. Stir in the flour, sugar, baking powder, salt, and cinnamon. Mix well.

4. Fill greased or lined muffin cups about halfway full.

5. Sprinkle the top of each muffin with a little sugar.

6. Bake at 400° for 18 to 20 minutes, or until golden brown.

Makes 12 muffins.

BLUEBERRY MUFFINS

Special Occasions

Mother's Day Breakfast in Bed

Every year we prepare our mom a special breakfast in bed. Even though mothers love everything their children do for them, we still try our very best to make this day special for her by starting it off with a real treat. Here's the menu we used last year, in case you need some suggestions.

*Fresh Fruit Cup**

*Blueberry Muffins**

*Pot of Hot Chocolate**

To make the *Fresh Fruit Cup*, we sliced fresh bananas, strawberries, and kiwi into a goblet, and garnished it with fresh blueberries. We also prepared a tray with a pretty placemat and cloth napkin, plus a tiny vase of wildflowers.

*Recipes are in this book.

There are lots of recipes for blueberry muffins, but this one is our favorite because it let's the real flavor of the blueberries come through.

HERE'S WHAT YOU NEED:

1 egg
1/2 cup milk
1/4 cup oil
1 1/2 cups flour
1/2 cup sugar
2 teaspoons baking powder
1/2 teaspoon salt
1 cup blueberries

Topping:

1/2 cup sugar
1/3 cup flour
1/2 teaspoon cinnamon
1/4 cup margarine, softened

HERE'S WHAT YOU DO:

1 Preheat oven to 400°.

2 Grease the bottom of muffin cups or use paper liners.

3 In a large bowl, beat the egg with a fork.

4 Add the milk and oil, and continue to stir.

5 Next, add all of the dry ingredients.

6 Mix the batter well, but be sure not to over-mix it. (Overmixing makes the muffins tough.) Carefully fold in the blueberries.

7 In a separate bowl, combine all of the ingredients for the topping. Mix until crumbly. This works best if you use your hands.

8 Fill each muffin cup about 2/3 full.

9 Sprinkle each muffin with about a tablespoon of topping.

10 Bake at 400° for 20 minutes, or until the muffins are plump and golden brown.

11 Serve warm with butter. These are good reheated in the microwave, too.

Makes about 10 to 12 muffins.

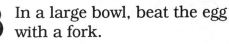

NANCY MERRILL'S ZUCCHINI BREAD

With Mrs. Merrill's recipe, it is easy to use up lots of extra zucchini from the garden. If you double this recipe, you can make extra loaves to have in the freezer. Then, some lazy morning, you can have a great breakfast treat!

HERE'S WHAT YOU NEED:

- 3 eggs
- 2 cups sugar
- 2 cups zucchini, grated and drained (squeeze out excess liquid)
- 1 cup oil
- 2 cups flour
- ¼ teaspoon baking soda
- ¼ teaspoon baking powder
- 1 teaspoon salt
- 3 teaspoons cinnamon
- 1 cup chopped nuts (optional)
- 3 teaspoons vanilla extract

HERE'S WHAT YOU DO:

1. Preheat oven to 350°.

2. In a large bowl, beat the eggs together.

3. Add the sugar, grated zucchini, and oil to the eggs.

4. Carefully sift all of the dry ingredients (flour, baking soda, baking powder, salt, cinnamon) into the mixture.

5. Add the chopped nuts and vanilla extract.

6. Mix everything together thoroughly.

7. Pour into two small loaf pans that have been greased.

8. Bake at 350° for 1 hour and 15 minutes.

9. Cool before removing loaf from pan.

Makes 2 loaves.

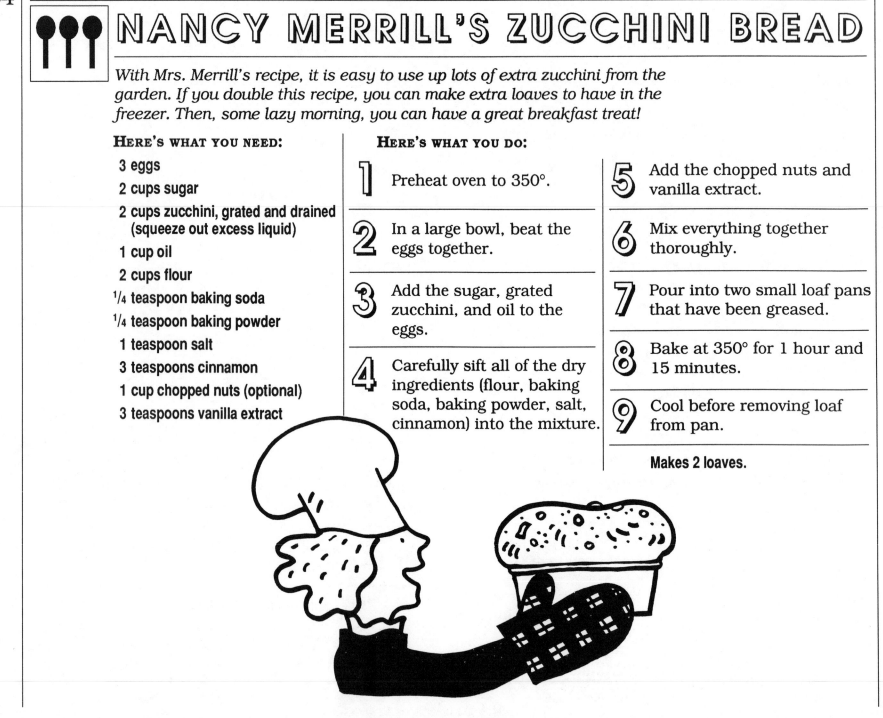

GRANDMA'S SOUR CREAM COFFEE CAKE

Great for a delicious breakfast, especially if you have friends over. This is sure to brighten any chilly morning and it is not difficult to make.

HERE'S WHAT YOU NEED:

- 1 stick margarine
- 1 cup sugar
- 2 eggs
- 1 cup sour cream
- 1 teaspoon baking soda
- 2 cups flour
- 1 teaspoon baking powder
- 1 teaspoon vanilla extract

Topping:

- 1/4 cup sugar
- 1 tablespoon cinnamon
- 2 tablespoons chopped nuts (walnuts or pecans are good)

HERE'S WHAT YOU DO:

1. Preheat oven to 350°.

2. Sift together baking powder, flour, and baking soda. Mix in sour cream. Set aside.

3. Cream margarine and sugar in a medium bowl. Add eggs, mix, and then add vanilla extract.

4. Combine all of the cake ingredients. Set aside.

5. In a small bowl, combine all of the topping ingredients and mix well. Set aside.

6. Put half of the cake batter into a greased 9" x 9" pan.

7. Sprinkle a layer of topping in the pan. Put in the rest of the batter. Then sprinkle the remaining topping to cover the cake.

8. Bake at 350° for 45 minutes. Check at 30 minutes to make sure that the topping isn't turning too brown. If it is, cover *very loosely* with a piece of tin foil, and continue baking until cake springs back when touched. Serve warm.

Makes enough for 12 people.

NUTRI·NOTE

An easy way to reduce fat and lower cholesterol is to use margarine instead of butter. Use tub margarine instead of bars of margarine and you'll be even better off.

BLUEBERRY BUCKLE

do you know?

It used to take a person one hour to milk six cows by hand. Today, with modern machines, one hundred cows can be milked in an hour.

Our whole family loves to have this for a special breakfast treat during blueberry season, but it's so good, you can enjoy it for an afternoon snack. It also makes a great dessert after dinner.

HERE'S WHAT YOU NEED:

3/4 **cup sugar**

1/4 **cup margarine, softened**

1 **egg**

1/2 **cup milk**

2 **cups flour**

2 **tablespoons baking powder**

1/2 **teaspoon salt**

2 **cups canned (drained) or fresh blueberries**

Topping:

1/2 **cup sugar**

1/3 **cup flour**

1/2 **teaspoon cinnamon**

1/4 **cup margarine, softened**

HERE'S WHAT YOU DO:

1 Preheat oven to 375°.

2 Wash and drain blueberries in a strainer.

3 Cream the margarine and sugar until light, then beat in the egg.

4 In a small mixing bowl, combine flour, baking powder, and salt. Alternately, add the flour mixture and the milk to the creamed margarine. Mix until well blended.

5 Gently fold in the blueberries. Spoon the batter into a greased 9" x 9" pan.

6 To make the topping, combine the sugar, flour, cinnamon, and soft margarine together. The mixture should be crumbly.

7 Sprinkle the topping over the batter evenly.

8 Bake at 350° for 45 minutes, or until cake springs back when touched.

9 Remove the cake from the oven, and let it cool slightly before cutting. This is best when it's served warm.

Makes enough for about 12 people.

GREAT LUNCHES

Whether you are at school watching the clock until lunchtime or at home on a busy Saturday, lunchtime is fun time. It provides a nice break in the day, a time to stretch and re-energize.

Lunch is a very flexible meal. You can choose from the recipes in this section as well as from the salad, snacks, or breakfast sections of the book. It really depends on your mood, your time limitations, and the ingredients you have in your house. If it is rainy and cold outside, a hot bowl of *Baked Onion Soup* and a *Tuna Melt* might prove to be the perfect pick-me-up. If you are planning a picnic with some friends, pack *Sarah's Chunky Chicken Salad* for a real treat.

Preparing lunch is easy and can be a lot of fun when you have friends over. Sometimes, if we can't find anything to do, we all start planning lunch early — baking some cookies or making soup. We have a good time in the morning working around the kitchen, listening to music, and joking with one another. Then, we treat ourselves to a great lunch! It's a nice way to spend part of the day.

SARAH'S CHUNKY CHICKEN SALAD

Sarah doesn't like tuna fish, so this is a great replacement. She makes it when we have leftover chicken, but you can quickly cook some boneless chicken to make this. It's delicious!

HERE'S WHAT YOU NEED:

³/₄ cup chicken, cooked and cut into large chunks

³/₄ cup celery, chopped

³/₄ cup green or red seedless grapes, halved

3 tablespoons red onion, minced

1 teaspoon dried tarragon

¹/₂ teaspoon curry powder (optional)

¹/₃ cup mayonnaise mixed with teaspoon Dijon-style mustard

¹/₂ cup raisins (optional)

Salt and pepper to taste

HERE'S WHAT YOU DO:

1 If you need to cook some chicken, place about two small boneless chicken breasts or equivalent dark meat in an oven-proof baking dish. Sprinkle with salt, pepper, and a few drops of lemon juice. Add about ¹/₄ cup water to dish. Bake at 350° for 20 to 25 minutes. Cool, cut into chunks, and then proceed with recipe.

2 In a large bowl, combine all of the ingredients and toss.

3 Chill before serving. Can be served as a salad with sliced tomatoes, a bunch of grapes, and some slices of avocado. Or, build a terrific sandwich on thick slices of whole wheat bread with your favorite sandwich toppings.

Makes enough for 2 people.

CLASSY COOKS

What does "optional" mean in a recipe? In many recipes, like salads and sandwiches, you can choose to add certain ingredients or leave them out. Optional means it's your choice; you can leave ingredients out without hurting the end result. If you don't like onions, you may decide to leave them out of all these recipes, but you can still make these recipes. When an ingredient is listed as optional, it usually means that the ingredient will change the flavor of the recipe, like the curry powder in *Sarah's Chunky Chicken Salad*. Curry powder has a very strong flavor, so some people don't like to cook with it. On the other hand, some people think it makes this salad really special, so you may want to try adding a little the first time. It's optional — or up to you!

FAMOUS TACO SALAD

Perfect for a large group of people or a party, we all love this. Our friend, Liz Harris, first introduced us to this recipe. It is a meal in itself.

HERE'S WHAT YOU NEED:

1 small head of iceberg lettuce, finely chopped

1½ pounds of hamburger meat

8 ounces of cheddar cheese, grated

1 pound of canned kidney beans, rinsed and drained

1 medium-sized onion, chopped

4 medium tomatoes, diced

1 tablespoon taco seasoning or add extra taco sauce

8 ounces Thousand Island salad dressing

1 tablespoon taco sauce

On the side: 1 package nacho chips

1 cup sour cream

1 cup salsa

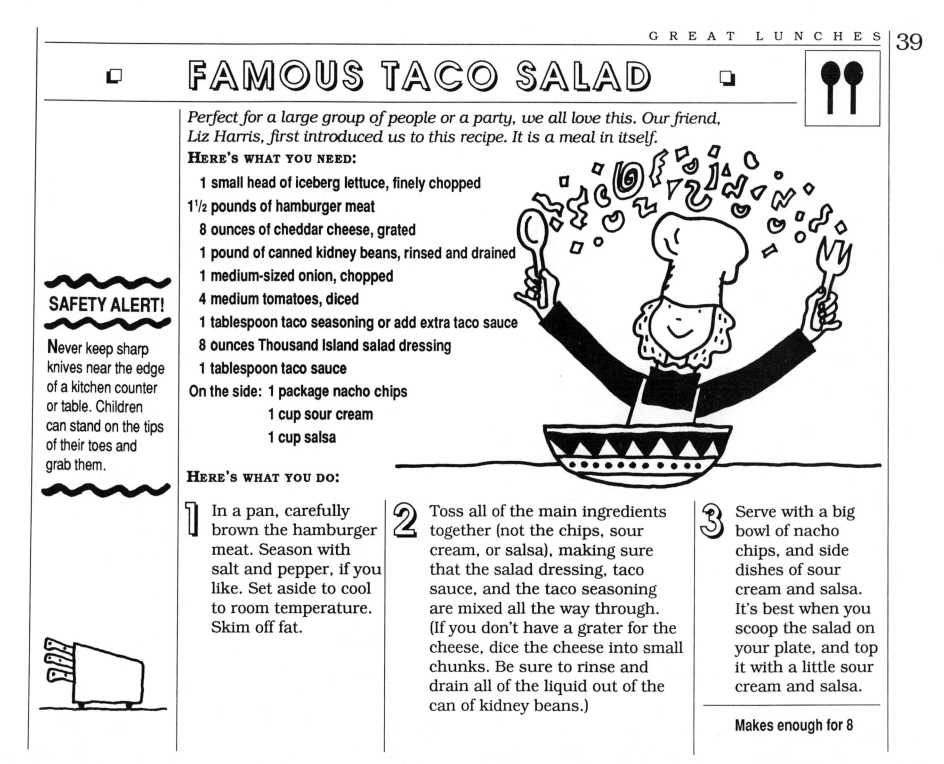

SAFETY ALERT!

Never keep sharp knives near the edge of a kitchen counter or table. Children can stand on the tips of their toes and grab them.

HERE'S WHAT YOU DO:

1 In a pan, carefully brown the hamburger meat. Season with salt and pepper, if you like. Set aside to cool to room temperature. Skim off fat.

2 Toss all of the main ingredients together (not the chips, sour cream, or salsa), making sure that the salad dressing, taco sauce, and the taco seasoning are mixed all the way through. (If you don't have a grater for the cheese, dice the cheese into small chunks. Be sure to rinse and drain all of the liquid out of the can of kidney beans.)

3 Serve with a big bowl of nacho chips, and side dishes of sour cream and salsa. It's best when you scoop the salad on your plate, and top it with a little sour cream and salsa.

Makes enough for 8

ZACH'S TUNA SURPRISE

This started out as plain tuna, but Zach added so many different ingredients that it is famous in our town. His friend, David Raabe, always asks him to make this.

HERE'S WHAT YOU NEED:

1 can (6.5 ounces) of white albacore tuna, drained
1/3 cup of mayonnaise
3 tablespoons of pickle relish
1/4 cup green stuffed olives, sliced
1/4 cup celery, chopped
1/4 cup red onion, chopped

HERE'S WHAT YOU DO:

1 Drain the water or oil from the can of tuna.

2 In a medium-sized bowl, combine all the ingredients.

3 Mix well.

4 Build your sandwich on your choice of bread. Top with lettuce and tomato. Or, serve salad on a plate with shredded lettuce and sliced tomatoes.

Makes about 2 large sandwiches.

TUNA MELT

Children have more taste buds than adults; as you age, you lose taste buds. That's why older people tend to use too much salt, which isn't a healthy thing to do. Maybe you can remind your parents not to use salt and to switch to other seasonings like pepper and herbs instead.

Oregano use fresh or dried with Tomato egg & cheese dishes!

Dill seeds & leaves in dishes of fish, lamb, stews, chicken, sauces, salad dressings & bread'!

Basil Fish, eggs, cheese, poultry, salads, meats, stuffings & spaghetti!

*Here's a real treat using **Zach's Tuna Surprise.***

HERE'S WHAT YOU NEED:

²⁄₃ **cup** *Zach's Tuna Surprise* **(see page 40)**

 1 **English muffin**

 2 **slices cheddar cheese, or your choice**

Tomato

Mayonnaise

HERE'S WHAT YOU DO:

1 Fork-split the English muffin and toast lightly.

2 Spread mayonnaise on English muffin.

3 Layer on tuna salad and slice of tomato on each half. Top with cheese.

4 Place in toaster oven on "top brown" option, or under broiler for 1 to 2 mintes until cheese is bubbly.

Makes 2 half open-faced sandwiches.

GREAT GAZPACHO

This is one of Sarah's specialties. Don't be turned away by the number of ingredients in this meal-in-a-bowl summer soup. It is easy to make and tastes wonderful.

HERE'S WHAT YOU NEED:

- 1 medium cucumber, chopped and seeded
- 3 tomatoes, peeled, seeded, diced
- 1 green pepper, seeded and chopped
- 1 onion, chopped
- ½ avocado, diced
- 4 cups tomato juice
- 4 basil leaves, chopped, or ½ teaspoon dried
- 2 teaspoons wine vinegar
- 3 tablespoons olive oil
- ½ teaspoon oregano, dried
- Salt to taste

HERE'S WHAT YOU DO:

1. Chop all of the vegetables except the avocado in a food processor (ask an adult to help you).

2. Combine the vegetables with the rest of the ingredients.

3. Stir and chill before serving.

4. Serve plain or pass bowls of chopped vegetables, *Homemade Seasoned Croutons* (see page 55), plain yogurt or sour cream, and chopped, fresh dill or basil.

Makes 4 servings.

CLASSY COOKS

How to peel a tomato:

1. Place tomato in boiling water for about one minute.
2. Take tomato directly from hot water to a bowl with cold water and ice.
3. Let tomato sit in cold water for one minute. Core and peel.

do·you·know?

A calorie measures the amount of energy stored in food. If you use up that energy through exercise, you won't gain weight. But, if you don't use that energy, it will be stored in your body as fat. Depending on the amount of activity kids engage in, girls ages 11 to 14 require an average of 2,200 calories for their daily needs. Boys ages 11 to 14 require an average of 2,700 calories per day. But it is better just to eat right and exercise a lot. That way you won't ever have to "count calories."

ONION SOUP

This summer Zach made this soup on a rainy day. It looked so beautiful (he made it in a small casserole dish instead of individual soup bowls) that we took pictures of it . . . . and it was delicious, too.

HERE'S WHAT YOU NEED:

- 5 **onions, peeled and sliced**
- 4 **tablespoons margarine**
- 3 **(12 ounce) cans beef broth**
- ¾ **cup water**
- ½ **teaspoon Worcestershire sauce**
- 1 **drop tabasco sauce**
- **Pepper**

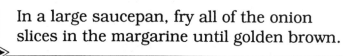

HERE'S WHAT YOU DO:

1 In a large saucepan, fry all of the onion slices in the margarine until golden brown.

get help

2 Pour the beef broth, water, Worcestershire sauce, tabasco sauce, and the pepper into a large pot. Add the fried onions.

3 Let simmer on medium heat for about an hour.

4 Serve with lots of grated cheese.

Makes 6 servings.

For baked onion soup:

If you prepare this in individual soup bowls as they do in restaurants, you MUST use special OVEN-PROOF BOWLS. If you don't have oven-proof bowls, simply use an oven-proof casserole dish. Follow the same directions, and then serve from the large casserole.

Here's what you do:

When the soup is made, pour it into the oven-proof bowls (or casserole dish). Take French bread slices and lightly toast them in the toaster. Put the toasted bread on top of the soup. Cover the toast with lots of grated cheese. Bake in the oven at 350° for about 10 minutes, or until cheese is bubbling and lightly browned. Be very careful removing the bowls from the oven. The soup is hot and so are the bowls.

SAFETY ALERT!

Always keep at least two pot holders handy when cooking. Otherwise, you may be tempted to grab a dish towel that won't protect you from burns and may hang down and catch on fire.

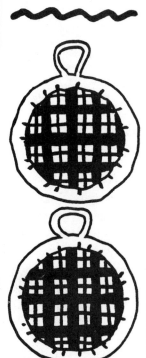

BEST SUMMER TOMATO SANDWICH

With fresh bread and beautiful garden tomatoes, this makes a great summer sandwich. If you don't have a garden, try growing a tomato plant in a flowerpot.

HERE'S WHAT YOU NEED:

1 loaf French bread

Tomatoes, sliced

Olive oil

Ground pepper

HERE'S WHAT YOU DO:

1 Cut bread lengthwise.

2 Layer bread with tomatoes.

3 Drizzle olive oil over tomatoes.

4 Sprinkle with pepper, and slice sandwich into wedges.

Makes 2 to 4 sandwiches.

AVOCADO SANDWICH

This is our mother's favorite summertime sandwich. We make it for her when she is working at home.

NUTRI·NOTE

Eating 8 ounces of potato chips is like adding 12 to 20 teaspoons of vegetable oil and a teaspoon of salt to an 8-ounce potato.

HERE'S WHAT YOU NEED:

Bread, your choice

Dijon-style mustard or mayonnaise

Cheese, your choice, sliced

Lettuce, red-leaf or your choice

Avocado, peeled and sliced

Red onion, sliced very thin

Sprouts

HERE'S WHAT YOU DO:

1 Spread two slices of bread with Dijon-style mustard or mayonnaise. This is especially good on whole wheat bread.

2 Layer cheese and lettuce on bread.

3 Add avocado and a slice of onion.

4 Top with sprouts. (Mom also likes to put a thin layer of chutney — a type of sweet, thick sauce that you can buy in the store — on this. You might try it this way, especially if you like sweet flavors.)

Makes as many as you like.

GARDEN FRESH SANDWICH

Sarah's friend, Michelle Richards, begs Sarah to make this for her at least once every summer.

HERE'S WHAT YOU NEED:

Bread, your choice

Mayonnaise or margarine

Cucumber, thinly sliced

Tomato, sliced

Cheese, your choice, sliced

HERE'S WHAT YOU DO:

1 Spread mayonnaise or margarine on two slices of bread.

2 Layer ingredients on bread.

Makes as many as you like.

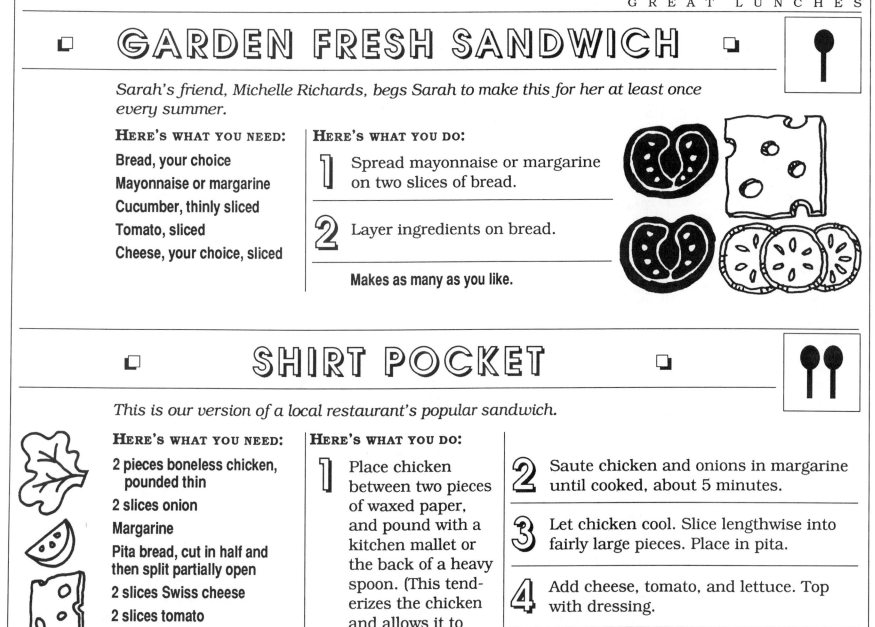

SHIRT POCKET

This is our version of a local restaurant's popular sandwich.

HERE'S WHAT YOU NEED:

2 pieces boneless chicken, pounded thin

2 slices onion

Margarine

Pita bread, cut in half and then split partially open

2 slices Swiss cheese

2 slices tomato

Lettuce

Thousand Island dressing

HERE'S WHAT YOU DO:

1 Place chicken between two pieces of waxed paper, and pound with a kitchen mallet or the back of a heavy spoon. (This tenderizes the chicken and allows it to cook faster.)

2 Saute chicken and onions in margarine until cooked, about 5 minutes.

3 Let chicken cool. Slice lengthwise into fairly large pieces. Place in pita.

4 Add cheese, tomato, and lettuce. Top with dressing.

Makes 2 large halves.

CLUB SANDWICH

CLASSY COOKS

Microwave Bacon. We like to microwave bacon, because it's an easy way to cook it without working around hot grease. Plus, if you use a special microwave pan, the fat falls beneath the bacon. There are many bacon substitutes available now, so try them since bacon is high in fat.

Here's what you do:

1. Place sliced bacon on microwave-approved pan.
2. Cover bacon with paper towels.
3. Microwave 6 pieces on high (100 percent power) for about 4 minutes, or follow your microwave instructions.
4. **HAVE AN ADULT REMOVE THE PAN FROM THE MICROWAVE, AS IT WILL HAVE HOT FAT IN IT. DON'T DO THIS YOURSELF.**
5. Blot extra fat from cooked bacon with paper towels.
6. If you don't have a microwave, we suggest that you ask an adult to prepare the bacon for you, as the hot fat is dangerous to work around.

get HELP

Sarah orders this sandwich at every restaurant we go to, but the ones we make at home are the best.

HERE'S WHAT YOU NEED:

3 slices bread, toasted

Mayonnaise

Turkey, sliced

Cheese, your choice, sliced

Bacon, cooked and drained

Lettuce

Tomato, sliced

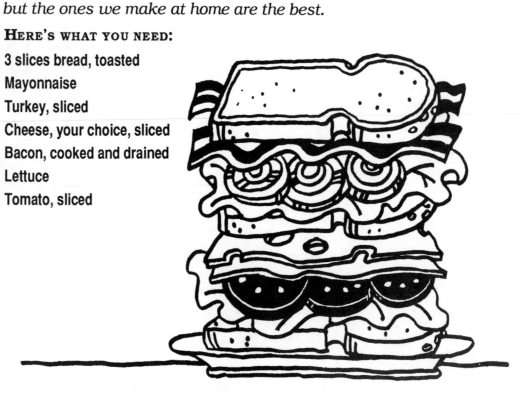

HERE'S WHAT YOU DO:

1 Spread mayonnaise on three slices of toast.

2 Layer the first slice with turkey and cheese.

3 Top with the second piece of toast (mayonnaise side up).

4 Layer second slice with bacon, lettuce, and tomato.

5 Top with third piece of toast (mayonnaise side down).

6 Cut sandwich in quarters. Serve with pickles and chips.

Makes as many as you like.

KIDS CAN!

Fourteen students from the University of Seattle covered 602 miles playing leapfrog. That is about the distance from St. Louis to Pittsburgh.

REUBEN SANDWICH

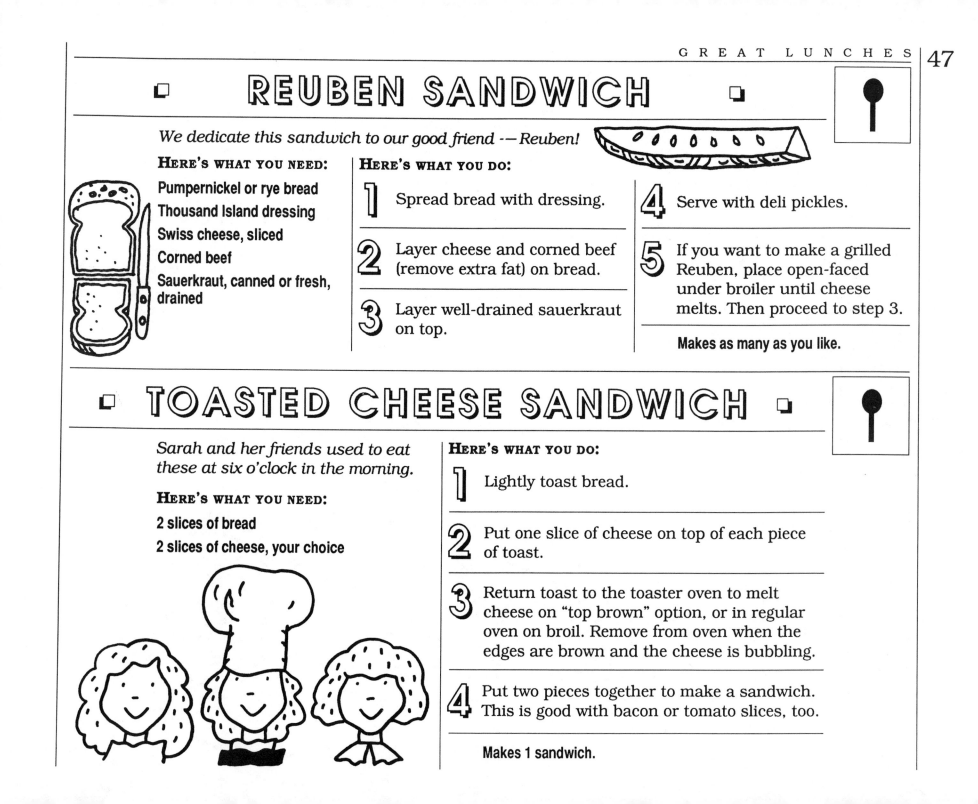

We dedicate this sandwich to our good friend -— Reuben!

HERE'S WHAT YOU NEED:

Pumpernickel or rye bread

Thousand Island dressing

Swiss cheese, sliced

Corned beef

Sauerkraut, canned or fresh, drained

HERE'S WHAT YOU DO:

1 Spread bread with dressing.

2 Layer cheese and corned beef (remove extra fat) on bread.

3 Layer well-drained sauerkraut on top.

4 Serve with deli pickles.

5 If you want to make a grilled Reuben, place open-faced under broiler until cheese melts. Then proceed to step 3.

Makes as many as you like.

TOASTED CHEESE SANDWICH

Sarah and her friends used to eat these at six o'clock in the morning.

HERE'S WHAT YOU NEED:

2 slices of bread

2 slices of cheese, your choice

HERE'S WHAT YOU DO:

1 Lightly toast bread.

2 Put one slice of cheese on top of each piece of toast.

3 Return toast to the toaster oven to melt cheese on "top brown" option, or in regular oven on broil. Remove from oven when the edges are brown and the cheese is bubbling.

4 Put two pieces together to make a sandwich. This is good with bacon or tomato slices, too.

Makes 1 sandwich.

ROAST BEEF SUPER SUB

Often our family "builds" subs on a Friday night before watching a movie.
For the best subs, use absolutely the freshest ingredients you can find.

CLASSY COOKS

It's up to you! With the *Roast Beef Super Sub* recipe it is entirely up to you to decide what goes on your sandwich. We have just tried to give you some ideas, but if you don't like an ingredient that we have included or you feel that an ingredient is missing, feel free to add or omit anything. This is true of many recipes, especially sandwiches and salads. Recipes are just starting points for your own good ideas.

HERE'S WHAT YOU NEED:

4 slices of fresh roast beef

3 slices of cheese, your choice

Mayonnaise, as much as you wish

Mustard, your choice

Lettuce

Tomato

Onion, thinly sliced

1 large grinder roll or fresh loaf of French bread

Dill pickles, thinly sliced

Green or red peppers, thinly sliced (optional)

Pepper

Olive oil

HERE'S WHAT YOU DO:

1 Cut the grinder roll in half lengthwise.

2 Spread on the mayonnaise and mustard.

3 Lay on the roast beef and cheese.

4 Top with the remaining ingredients or any others of your choosing.

5 Sprinkle a few drops of olive oil on top of the vegetables.

Makes one very large sandwich.

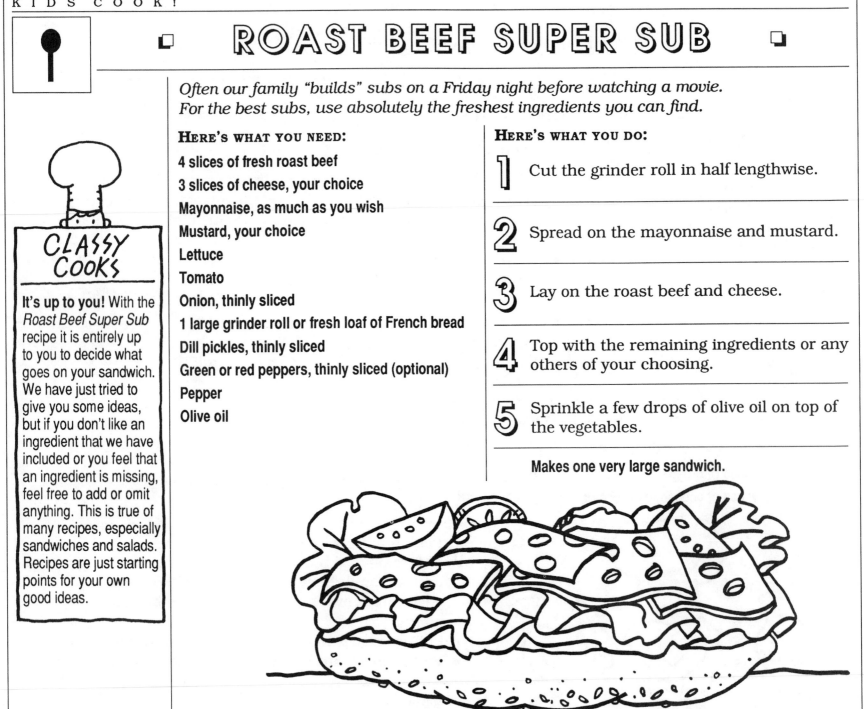

STUFFED RAISIN BAGELS

If you want something different, something good for you, and good tasting, then try this. We like it best made with cinnamon-raisin bagels, but you can use whatever you like, or simply serve it like a salad. You can also vary the ingredients, leaving out something you don't like or adding chunks of leftover chicken or grapes.

HERE'S WHAT YOU NEED:

1 cinnamon-raisin bagel, or your choice

$3/4$ cup shredded Swiss or cheddar cheese

$3/4$ cup carrots, thinly sliced or shredded

$1/4$ cup chopped walnuts or pecans

$1/4$ cup raisins

1 apple, diced (peeling is optional)

Mayonnaise

HERE'S WHAT YOU DO:

1. Combine all ingredients except bagel, adding enough mayonnaise to moisten and hold the salad together.

2. Split and toast the bagel.

3. Pile high on bagel halves for open-faced sandwiches, or serve on a plate as salad with toasted bagel on the side.

Makes 2 open-faced sandwiches.

BAGEL PIZZAS

A nice change from the everyday sandwich, this makes a good lunch or afternoon snack.

HERE'S WHAT YOU NEED:

1 bagel, split in half

6 tablespoons of tomato sauce or spaghetti sauce

6 slices of your favorite type of cheese (cheddar, Swiss, mozzarella, etc.)

HERE'S WHAT YOU DO:

1. Preheat oven to 350°.

2. Put about 3 tablespoons of tomato sauce on each half of the bagel.

3. Cover the sauce with three slices of cheese on each half.

4. Place in a baking dish or on a cookie sheet. Put in oven at 350° for about 10 minutes, or until cheese is bubbling and melted.

Makes 2 half bagels.

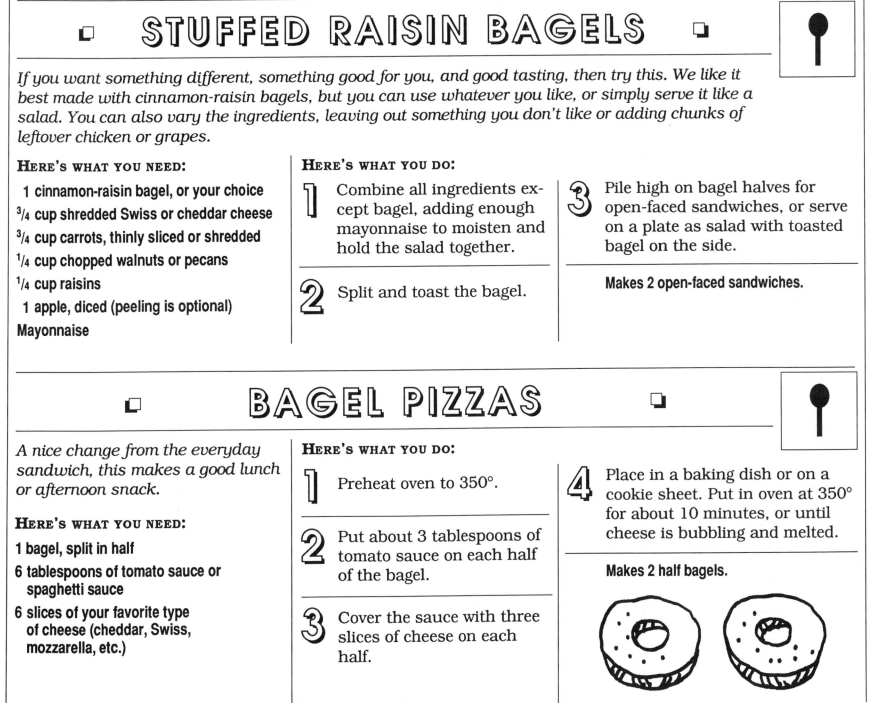

EGG SALAD SANDWICH

When our friend, Sarah Novick, used to come to our house, she would eat nothing but this egg salad.

HERE'S WHAT YOU NEED:

4 to 5 eggs, hard-boiled

1/2 cup celery, chopped

1/2 cup green olives, sliced

1/4 cup red onion (optional)

1/2 cup mayonnaise

1 teaspoon Dijon-style mustard (optional)

Salt and pepper to taste

CLASSY COOKS

How to hard-boil an egg:

1. Place eggs in a saucepan so that eggs are not on top of each other. Add a half teaspoon of salt and enough water to cover the eggs.

2. Set the saucepan on high heat until the water comes to a simmer (when bubbles begin to come to the surface).

3. Lower heat and continue to simmer the eggs for 15 to 20 minutes.

5. Drain the hot water immediately. Cover with cold water. This will make the eggs easier to peel when they are completely cool.

HERE'S WHAT YOU DO:

1. See instructions for how to hard-boil an egg.

2. Peel and mash eggs, using a fork or potato masher.

3. Add remaining ingredients and mix gently.

4. Chill before serving. Make a sandwich on any type of bread and top with very crisp lettuce. If you like pumpernickel bread, it goes great with egg salad. You can also serve on a plate with orange sections on the side.

Makes 3 to 4 servings.

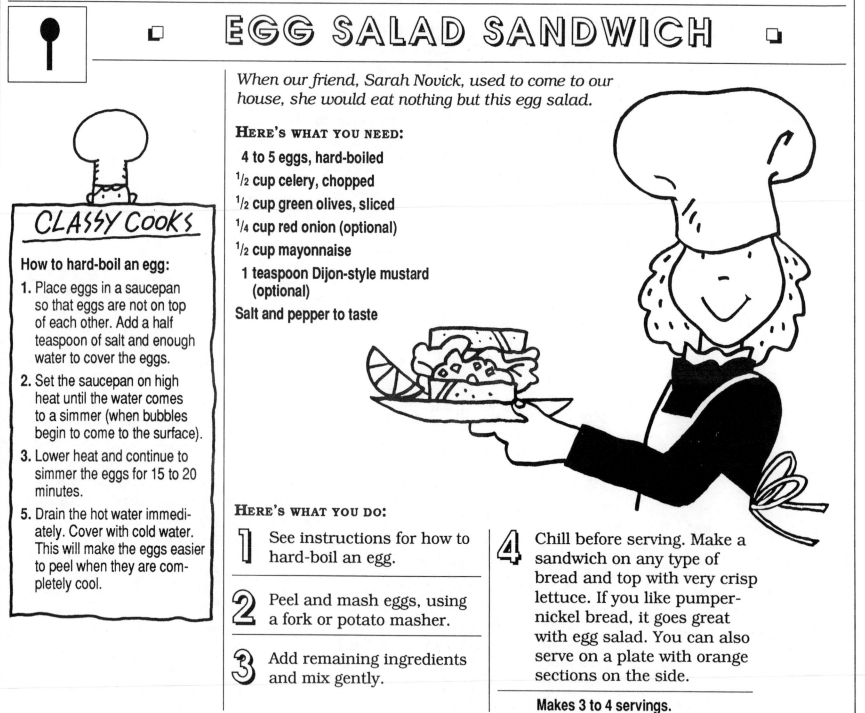

SUPER SALADS

Making a salad can be lots of fun if you are feeling creative, because just about anything and everything goes! You can plan a salad with lots of contrasts of color and texture, as well as contrasts in flavor. You can make a mixed-together salad like *Best Potato Salad*, or you can work on perfecting a beautifully arranged salad like *Fresh Antipasto* where each ingredient is displayed for appetite appeal. If you have leftover meats and vegetables, a variation on our *Cobb Salad* is a perfect, creative solution to those leftover blues.

There is nothing better tasting than using your own homegrown vegetables in a tossed salad. If you have different herbs such as basil, dill, or parsley in your garden or growing indoors in flowerpots, you can sprinkle them onto any type of salad to add a little pep.

If someone in your family is trying to cut down on fat and cholesterol, substitute non-fat plain yogurt for mayonnaise or try some low-cholesterol or low-fat mayonnaise instead. Salads are healthy additions to any meal, or they can be served as meals in themselves. As you can tell, salads are one of our favorite foods. We hope you like these recipes.

TERRIFIC TOMATO SALAD

If you like garden fresh tomatoes, then you'll love this very easy-to-make salad.

HERE'S WHAT YOU NEED:

- 3 to 4 tomatoes, sliced
- 2 tablespoons olive oil
- 2 teaspoons vinegar, any flavor such as balsamic, tarragon, or cider
- 1 tablespoon red onion, chopped
- 1/2 teaspoon basil, dried or 1 tablespoon fresh
- 1/4 teaspoon salt
- 1/8 teaspoon sugar
- 1/4 cup mozzarella cheese, shredded
- Freshly ground pepper

HERE'S WHAT YOU DO:

1 Combine all of the ingredients in a bowl except the sliced tomatoes and mozzarella.

2 Mix well with a whisk.

3 Arrange the tomatoes on a plate. Sprinkle with mozzarella cheese and some freshly ground pepper. When it is time to serve, pour the dressing over the sliced tomatoes.

Makes enough for 6 people.

NUTRI-NOTE

No foods are "good" or "bad;" they all fit into the scheme of the four food groups. The problem comes when we eat too much of one thing and not enough of something else.

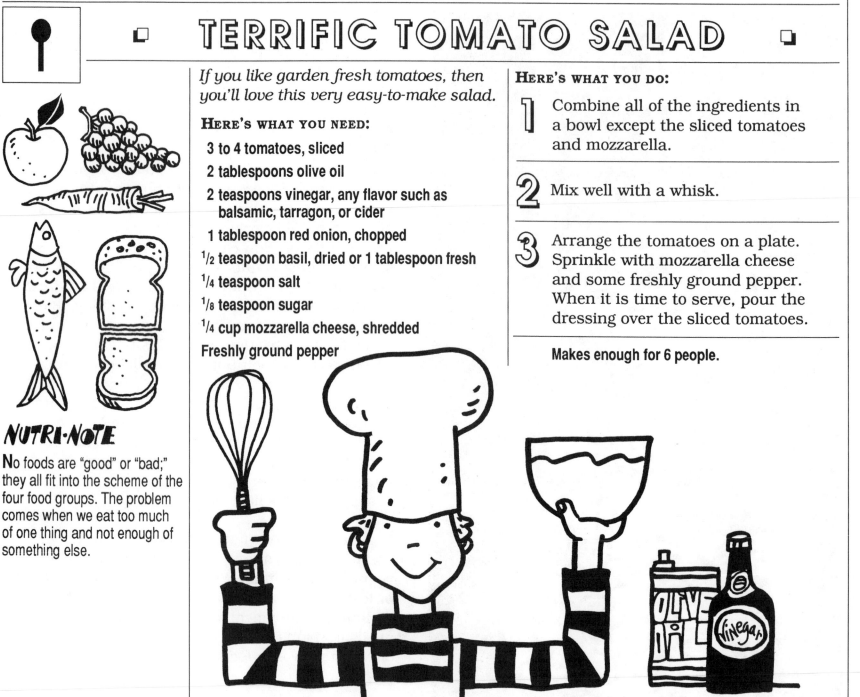

CUCUMBER SALAD

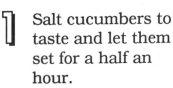

NUTRI·NOTE

No more than 30 percent of your calories should come from fat. Even teens should be aware of their fat intake. Remember it is harder to change a bad habit than it is to start a good habit.

Our Grandma Golde used to keep a glass container of this in the refrigerator on hot summer days. Of course, it is best when you make it with fresh cucumbers from the garden, but any cucumber will do! Somehow, this always tasted very special to us.

HERE'S WHAT YOU NEED:

2 cucumbers, peeled and sliced thin

1/2 cup mild onion, sliced thin

1/4 cup water

2 tablespoons sugar

1/2 cup white vinegar

Salt to taste

HERE'S WHAT YOU DO:

1 Salt cucumbers to taste and let them set for a half an hour.

2 Rinse cucumbers well under cold water and pat dry.

3 Add the onions and mix well.

4 In a separate bowl, combine the water, sugar, and vinegar.

5 Pour this mixture over the cucumbers and onions. Cover and refrigerate for at least 4 hours.

6 To serve, lift cucumbers and onions out of the marinade onto a pretty dish.

Makes enough for about 4 people.

FRESH & DELICIOUS TOSSED SALAD

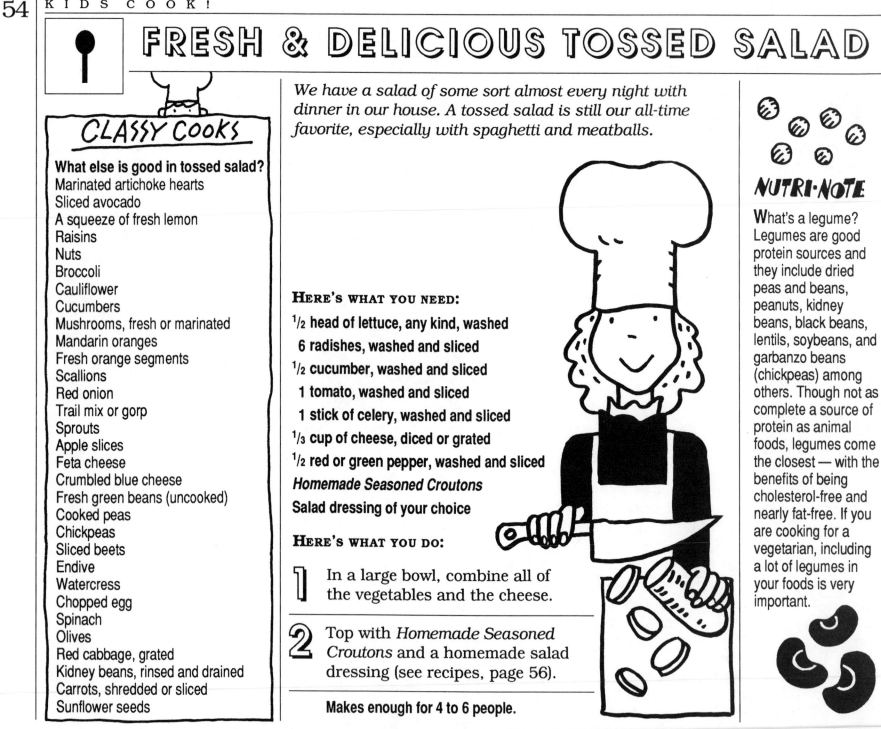

CLASSY COOKS

What else is good in tossed salad?
Marinated artichoke hearts
Sliced avocado
A squeeze of fresh lemon
Raisins
Nuts
Broccoli
Cauliflower
Cucumbers
Mushrooms, fresh or marinated
Mandarin oranges
Fresh orange segments
Scallions
Red onion
Trail mix or gorp
Sprouts
Apple slices
Feta cheese
Crumbled blue cheese
Fresh green beans (uncooked)
Cooked peas
Chickpeas
Sliced beets
Endive
Watercress
Chopped egg
Spinach
Olives
Red cabbage, grated
Kidney beans, rinsed and drained
Carrots, shredded or sliced
Sunflower seeds

We have a salad of some sort almost every night with dinner in our house. A tossed salad is still our all-time favorite, especially with spaghetti and meatballs.

HERE'S WHAT YOU NEED:

½ **head of lettuce, any kind, washed**
6 **radishes, washed and sliced**
½ **cucumber, washed and sliced**
1 **tomato, washed and sliced**
1 **stick of celery, washed and sliced**
⅓ **cup of cheese, diced or grated**
½ **red or green pepper, washed and sliced**
Homemade Seasoned Croutons
Salad dressing of your choice

HERE'S WHAT YOU DO:

1 In a large bowl, combine all of the vegetables and the cheese.

2 Top with *Homemade Seasoned Croutons* and a homemade salad dressing (see recipes, page 56).

Makes enough for 4 to 6 people.

NUTRI·NOTE

What's a legume? Legumes are good protein sources and they include dried peas and beans, peanuts, kidney beans, black beans, lentils, soybeans, and garbanzo beans (chickpeas) among others. Though not as complete a source of protein as animal foods, legumes come the closest — with the benefits of being cholesterol-free and nearly fat-free. If you are cooking for a vegetarian, including a lot of legumes in your foods is very important.

HOMEMADE SEASONED CROUTONS

Storebought croutons are convenient and they make a good snack right out of the box, but if you want a real tasty treat, make some homemade croutons with any kind of leftover bread.

HERE'S WHAT YOU NEED:

2 **cups of bread cubes made from stale bread, a mixture of many kinds is best**

1/2 **cup margarine**

1 **clove of garlic, minced**

2 **tablespoons grated Parmesan cheese**

A pinch of dried herbs such as dill, tarragon, oregano, and basil

HERE'S WHAT YOU DO:

1 Preheat the oven to 350°.

2 Cut the bread into medium-sized cubes, and dry them in the oven on a cookie sheet for 5 minutes.

3 Melt the margarine and saute the garlic until soft. Place the bread cubes in a large bowl. Pour the melted margarine over the bread cubes and add remaining ingredients. Toss well.

4 Return to the oven on cookie sheet and bake for about 3 minutes, until lightly browned.

5 Serve cooled croutons on salads or soups. Store them in a covered container in the refrigerator.

Makes 2 cups.

THOUSAND ISLAND DRESSING

Here's a favorite that can dress up simple lettuce and tomato.

HERE'S WHAT YOU NEED:

1 cup mayonnaise

1/4 cup ketchup or chili sauce

2 tablespoons pickle relish

1 tablespoon horseradish (optional)

HERE'S WHAT YOU DO:

1 Combine all ingredients. Mix well.

Makes 1 1/4 cups salad dressing.

BASIC VINAIGRETTE DRESSING

For the simplest dressing, just add vinegar and oil in these proportions.

HERE'S WHAT YOU NEED:

1/2 cup wine vinegar

1 teaspoon salt

Dash of pepper

1 1/2 cups vegetable oil or salad oil

HERE'S WHAT YOU DO:

1 Whisk all ingredients together, or shake them together in a small jar.

Makes 2 cups.

Options: Add 2 tablespoons Dijon-style mustard for a *Mustard Vinaigrette*.

Substitute 1/2 cup lemon juice for part of the vinegar, for a *Lemon Vinaigrette*.

Add 1 clove garlic, minced, for a *Garlic Vinaigrette*.

Substitute any kind of flavored vinegar that you wish for a nice change.

SALAD BAR

Just about everyone has a favorite salad bar at a special restaurant. Here is a salad bar you can create at home. It is fun to do this when you have some friends over or when you and your family are watching a favorite show or football game on T.V.

HERE'S WHAT YOU NEED:

Lettuce, washed and shredded

Tomatoes, washed and sliced

Cucumbers, washed, peeled, and sliced

Green and red peppers, washed and sliced

Cheese, grated or diced

Chickpeas, drained

Carrots, washed and peeled, grated or sliced

Croutons

Raisins

An assortment of salad dressings

HERE'S WHAT YOU DO:

1 Prepare each ingredient as directed.

2 Put each ingredient in a bowl and make a line going along the side of a counter. Set up the order of ingredients by the order in which we listed them.

3 Add any other things to your salad bar from the list of salad options (see page 54) or from your own great ideas.

Makes enough for as many as you want.

BROCCOLI BACON SALAD

This is a wonderful winter salad that is sure to be popular with your family and friends.

HERE'S WHAT YOU NEED:

1 bunch of broccoli, washed

1 cup raisins

1/4 cup sunflower seeds

1/2 pound bacon, cooked

1/2 to 3/4 cup mayonnaise

2 teaspoons vinegar

1 tablespoon sugar

HERE'S WHAT YOU DO:

1 Wash broccoli carefully and dry. Cut the florets off the stems, and then cut into small bite-sized pieces.

2 Cook the bacon according to the directions on page 46. Blot and cool. Then, break into small pieces. Add to the broccoli.

3 Add the raisins and sunflower seeds to broccoli.

4 Mix together the mayonnaise, vinegar, and sugar in a separate bowl. Pour over the broccoli and toss all together. Serve in a pretty bowl.

Makes enough for 4 people.

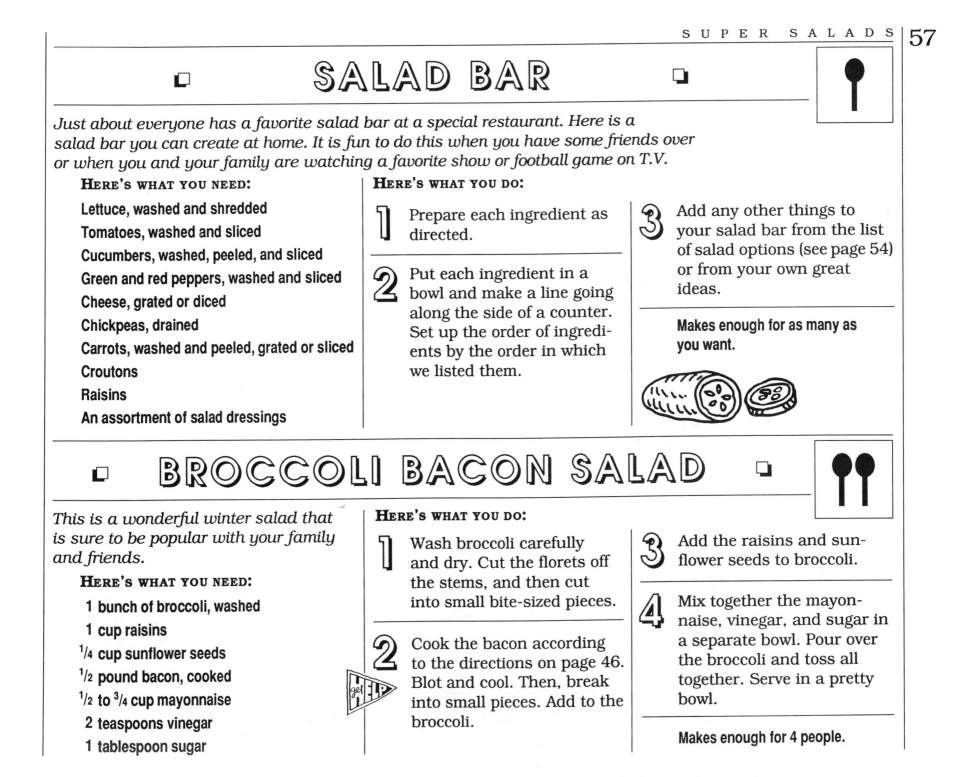

FRESH ANTIPASTO

We think that antipasto is a fun salad to make and eat. It is an arranged salad — usually served on a big platter. Pass the platter around and your friends and family may help themselves to what they want.

HERE'S WHAT YOU NEED:

Lettuce, washed and shredded

Black olives

Green olives

Bermuda onion, thickly sliced

Vinegar, balsamic is best

Olive oil

Ham, sliced and rolled up

Salami, cut in chunks

Pepperoni, sliced (optional)

Different types of cheese, cut in chunks (provolone, Swiss, and cheddar are good)

Marinated artichoke hearts

Pickled peppers

Red pepper, washed and sliced

HERE'S WHAT YOU DO:

1 Spread the shredded lettuce on a large platter.

2 Set aside the olives, Bermuda onion, vinegar, and oil. Arrange the remaining ingredients on top of the bed of lettuce, so that they are next to one another but not mixed together.

3 Sprinkle the olives and onions on top as a garnish. Don't toss the salad. Let people serve themselves on small salad plates, taking what they want.

4 Pass the oil and vinegar.

Makes enough for 6 people.

KIDS CAN!

Guy Stewart of Ohio jumped 130,077 jumps on a pogo stick.

COBB SALAD

This salad became a family favorite when Zachary started ordering it in restaurants. Soon he was also making it at home. It is a meal in itself and is great to cook when you are in charge of getting dinner or when you want a special lunch.

HERE'S WHAT YOU NEED:

Egg, hard-boiled

1 whole boneless breast of chicken

Onion, chopped

Vegetable oil

Lettuce, washed, dried, shredded

Tomato, diced

Blue cheese, crumbled

Salad dressing, your choice

Bacon (optional)

HERE'S WHAT YOU DO:

1 Follow the directions on page 50 to hard-boil your egg.

2 Saute the chicken in a frying pan with some oil and the chopped onion. (If you place it between pieces of waxed paper and pound it with a heavy spoon before sauteing, it will cook faster and be more tender.) Cook through until lightly browned. When cooled, cut into chunks.

3 In a large dish or shallow bowl, prepare a bed of shredded lettuce.

4 Arrange the remaining ingredients except the salad dressing in small sections of each ingredient. Do not toss together.

5 Serve with lots of salad dressing (we've always thought that blue cheese dressing goes best with this salad).

Makes 1 big salad for a full meal, or 2 smaller lunch salads.

A WHALE OF A FRUIT SALAD

This is one of Zachary's favorite specialties. He has made it for parties and just for fun, too. In addition to the whale shape, a basket shape can be made — just carve the top off in two large pieces, leaving a handle for the basket. The basket can have a decorative border.

HERE'S WHAT YOU NEED:

1 large watermelon, as oval as possible

2 cantaloupe melons

2 honeydew melons

Green grapes, seedless, washed

Red grapes, seedless, washed

3 kiwis, peeled and sliced

2 quarts of strawberries, washed, hulled, and halved

2 pints of blueberries, washed

HERE'S WHAT YOU DO:

1 Carve the watermelon. (See next page.)

2 Using a melon-ball scoop, preferably with two different sized scoops, take out the insides of the watermelon. Place the watermelon balls in a large bowl. With a normal-sized spoon, scrape out any extra watermelon that might be left on the sides. Save this to nibble on.

3 Cut the cantaloupe and honeydew melons in half, and remove the seeds. Again, using the scoop, scoop out balls of melon. Place in the bowl with the watermelon balls.

4 Pick the grapes off the stem and place in the bowl.

5 Pour in the cleaned strawberries and blueberries.

6 Carefully toss the entire salad and fill the whale.

7 Before serving, peel and slice the kiwis. Garnish the salad with kiwi slices.

8 Prepare this salad as close to serving time as possible. Refrigerate until ready to serve.

Serves about 20 people.

HOW TO CARVE A WHALE:

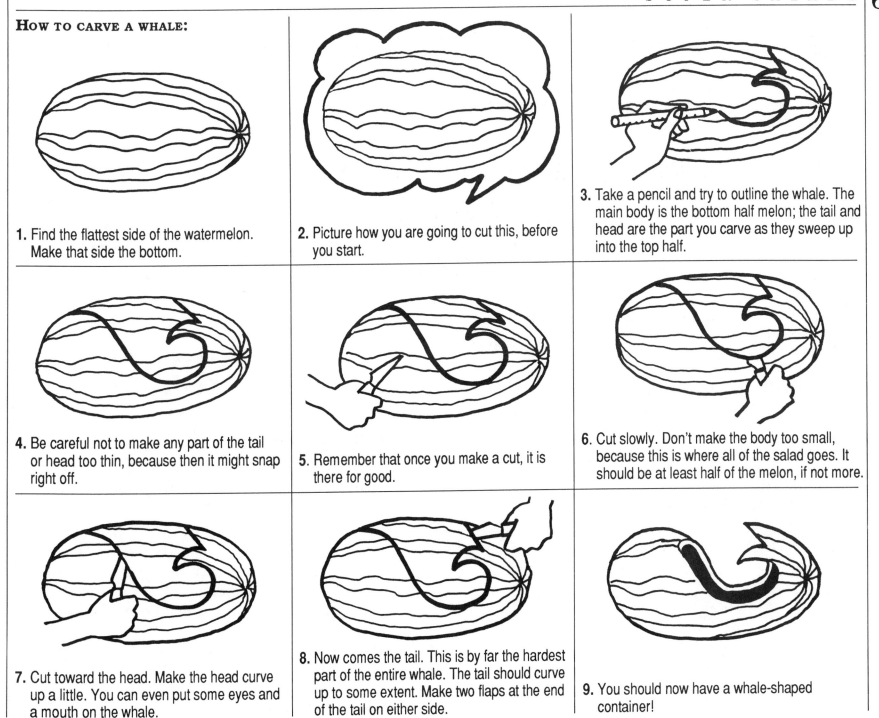

1. Find the flattest side of the watermelon. Make that side the bottom.

2. Picture how you are going to cut this, before you start.

3. Take a pencil and try to outline the whale. The main body is the bottom half melon; the tail and head are the part you carve as they sweep up into the top half.

4. Be careful not to make any part of the tail or head too thin, because then it might snap right off.

5. Remember that once you make a cut, it is there for good.

6. Cut slowly. Don't make the body too small, because this is where all of the salad goes. It should be at least half of the melon, if not more.

7. Cut toward the head. Make the head curve up a little. You can even put some eyes and a mouth on the whale.

8. Now comes the tail. This is by far the hardest part of the entire whale. The tail should curve up to some extent. Make two flaps at the end of the tail on either side.

9. You should now have a whale-shaped container!

□ APRICOT ORANGE JELLO™ MOLD □

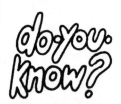

Even if you don't think you like Jello™ molds, this one is absolutely delicious and it seems that nearly everyone likes it. It is not hard to make, either.

do you know?

What's the difference between Jello™ and gelatin? Nothing — they are the same thing. Jello™ is a trademark for a brand of gelatin made by the General Foods Corporation. It's the same as asking someone to pass you a Kleenex™ when you really are asking for a tissue. Sometimes it's fun to amuse yourself by thinking of other products we call by their popular brand names instead of by what they really are.

HERE'S WHAT YOU NEED:

1 large package (6 ounces) orange gelatin

1 can (11 ounces) mandarin oranges

1 can (11 ounces) apricot halves, peeled

4 cups liquid (use liquid from apricots and oranges and add water to equal 4 cups)

1 pint sour cream or plain yogurt

HERE'S WHAT YOU DO:

1 Dissolve gelatin in 4 cups hot liquid, as noted above.

2 Chill until fairly firm.

3 In either a special gelatin mold or in a 9" x 9" pan, arrange the ingredients in layers as follows: 1 layer of gelatin; 1 layer of apricots; 1 layer of gelatin; 1 layer of sour cream; 1 layer of gelatin; 1 layer of mandarin oranges; last layer of gelatin.

4 Return to refrigerator to set firmly. Either unmold with the help of an adult or spoon out to serve.

Makes enough for 8 people.

MACARONI SALAD

We always think of this as a summer salad, but actually it is great any time of year and almost any time of day (well, not really for breakfast!). Any leftovers make a good after school snack.

HERE'S WHAT YOU NEED:

- 8 ounces bow-tie macaroni, or other type of macaroni
- 3 carrots
- 3 celery sticks, sliced
- 1 small red onion, chopped
- 1/2 cup green olives, sliced
- 1/2 cup black olives, sliced
- 1/2 cup green pepper, diced
- 1/2 cup red pepper, diced
- 3/4 cup mayonnaise
- 2 tablespoons cider vinegar
- 1 teaspoon tarragon (optional)
- 1 tablespoon sour cream or non-fat yogurt

HERE'S WHAT YOU DO:

1. Boil macaroni according to directions on box or until the macaroni is soft, but not mushy. Pour into a strainer, drain, and rinse with cold water. Set aside to cool and drain very thoroughly.

2. Wash, peel, and slice the carrots. Wash all of the vegetables and either slice, dice, or chop them. Put all of the vegetables in a large bowl.

3. In a different bowl, whisk together the mayonnaise, vinegar, tarragon, and sour cream. Once this is well blended, pour it over the vegetables.

4. Carefully empty the macaroni into the large bowl containing the vegetable mixture. Gently mix together making sure that the macaroni and the vegetables are coated with the sauce. Chill before serving.

Makes enough for 4 to 6 people.

Options: If you don't like a certain vegetable that we have included in this recipe, or you don't have that vegetable in your house, just skip it. Experiment a little and add some different ingredients of your own.

VEGGIES AND SHELLS

This is the kind of recipe where you can add what you like and leave out the rest. Here is one way that we really do like this!

HERE'S WHAT YOU NEED:

1 box (8 ounces) of small shell macaroni

2 small scallions, sliced thin

3 tablespoons olive oil or vegetable oil

2 tablespoons flavored vinegar (balsamic, raspberry, or tarragon)

1 teaspoon Dijon-style mustard

3/4 cup mayonnaise, or part non-fat plain yogurt

2 small zucchini, sliced thin

1 red bell pepper, cut in thin strips

Salt and pepper to taste

1 cup Greek-styled olives (for garnish)

2 tablespoons grated Parmesan cheese (for garnish)

HERE'S WHAT YOU DO:

1 Boil pasta according to package directions. Drain

2 Add scallions and olive oil to hot, drained pasta. Mix thoroughly and set aside to cool.

3 Add remaining vegetables except olives, and toss.

4 Whisk together vinegar, mustard, and mayonnaise in a small bowl. Pour over salad and toss.

5 Taste and add salt and pepper if necessary. If it is too vinegary for your taste, add a pinch of sugar.

6 Chill well before serving. Pour into a pretty serving bowl.

7 Sprinkle with Parmesan cheese and garnish with olives.

Makes enough for 12 people.

SAFETY ALERT!

If a baby is choking, let him cough up what is lodged in his throat. If he is choking, but not coughing, or has stopped breathing, turn him over and smack him on the back. Call immediately for emergency help.

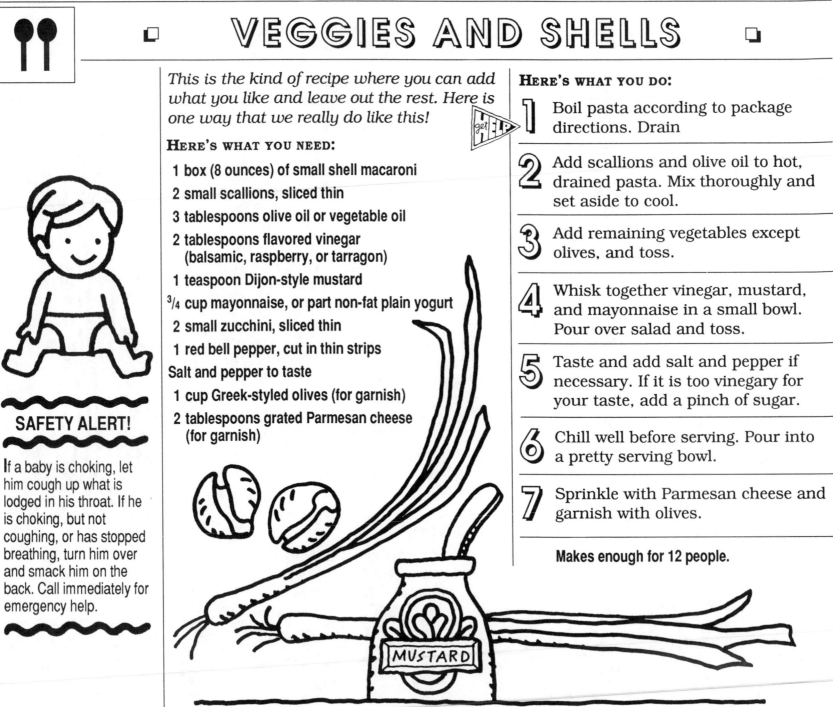

MUSTARD

GARDEN FRESH TUNA PASTA SALAD

This combines the best of two worlds — macaroni salad and tuna salad. It's easy to make, and you don't have to follow the ingredients or amounts exactly. Use this recipe to begin to build your own favorite salad.

HERE'S WHAT YOU NEED:

8 ounces elbow macaroni

1 cup mayonnaise

3 tablespoons red wine vinegar

1 tablespoon fresh basil, chopped
  (or 1 teaspoon dried basil)

1 clove garlic, minced

1 teaspoon salt

¼ teaspoon pepper

1 can (6.5 to 12.5 ounces) of tuna, drained

1 cup cherry tomatoes, quartered

½ cup red onion, thinly sliced

½ cup green olives, sliced

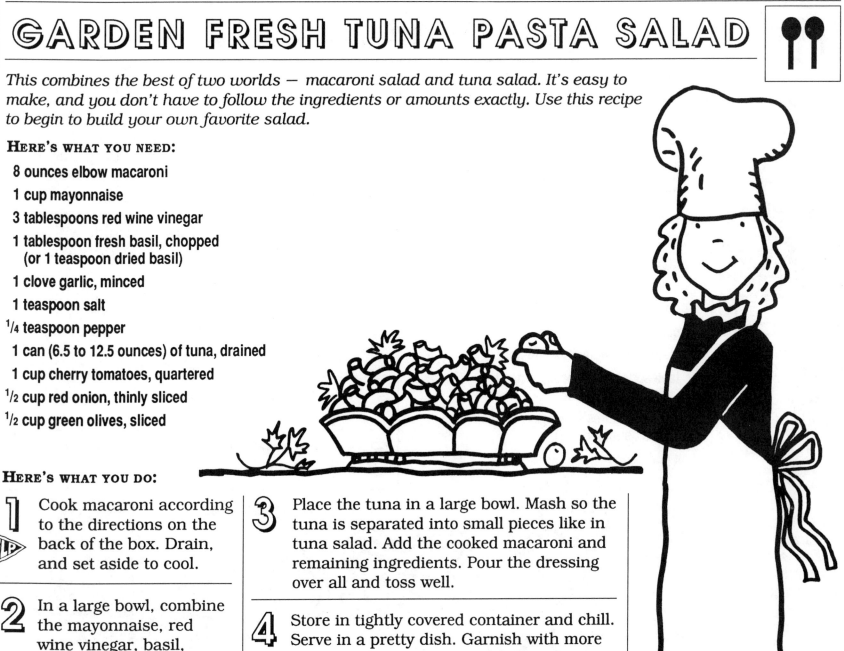

HERE'S WHAT YOU DO:

1 Cook macaroni according to the directions on the back of the box. Drain, and set aside to cool.

get HELP

2 In a large bowl, combine the mayonnaise, red wine vinegar, basil, garlic, salt, and pepper. Whisk together.

3 Place the tuna in a large bowl. Mash so the tuna is separated into small pieces like in tuna salad. Add the cooked macaroni and remaining ingredients. Pour the dressing over all and toss well.

4 Store in tightly covered container and chill. Serve in a pretty dish. Garnish with more cherry tomatoes or pieces of parsley.

Makes about 8 cups.

BEST POTATO SALAD

There are a lot of recipes for potato salad, but we think this is the best. It is a favorite summertime salad — great for lunch or dinner, and perfect on a picnic.

HERE'S WHAT YOU NEED:

10 small new (red) potatoes

2 tablespoons tarragon vinegar, or other vinegar

2 tablespoons olive oil

2 carrots, peeled and sliced thin

1/2 green pepper, diced

1/2 small red onion

3/4 cup green olives, halved

3/4 cup mayonnaise

2 teaspoons Dijon-style mustard

1 tablespoon fresh basil, minced (or 1 teaspoon dried)

1 tablespoon fresh tarragon, minced (or 1 teaspoon dried)

Salt and pepper

HERE'S WHAT YOU DO:

1 Cook potatoes in boiling water until they feel tender when punctured with a fork, about 20 minutes.

get HELP

2 Drain and put in big bowl. Sprinkle with the vinegar and olive oil. Set aside to cool.

3 Dice potatoes into large chunks. Add the carrots, green pepper, onion, and olives.

4 In a separate bowl, combine the mayonnaise, mustard, and herbs. Whisk together well. Pour over the potatoes and vegetables and toss well. Chill.

5 Serve in a pretty bowl with a few sprinkles of paprika for color.

Makes enough for 10 people.

What's the difference between foods labelled "lite" and "low-fat"? "Lite" means that the product is lower in calories, salt, or sugar than traditionally packaged foods, supposedly by at least 25 percent. "Low-fat" foods are those which contain less than 10 percent fat per serving.

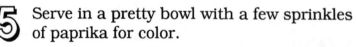

GREAT COLE SLAW

What's a summertime picnic without cole slaw? In our family, every Memorial Day means the first picnic of the year and the first cole slaw, too.

HERE'S WHAT YOU NEED:

1 small head of cabbage, shredded

1 cup green pepper, diced

1/2 cup carrot, grated

1/2 cup mild onion, diced

1 cup mayonnaise

2 tablespoons vinegar

1/4 cup celery seed

2 teaspoons sugar

3 tablespoons sour cream or non-fat yogurt

HERE'S WHAT YOU DO:

1 Shred cabbage and place in large bowl.

2 Add remaining vegetables to bowl and toss.

3 In a small bowl, combine the mayonnaise, vinegar, celery seed, sugar, and sour cream. Mix well and pour over cabbage and vegetables. Toss well and refrigerate several hours before serving.

Makes enough for 10 people.

NUTRI-NOTE

Skinless turkey contains about one-third less fat than skinless chicken.

TORTELLINI SALAD

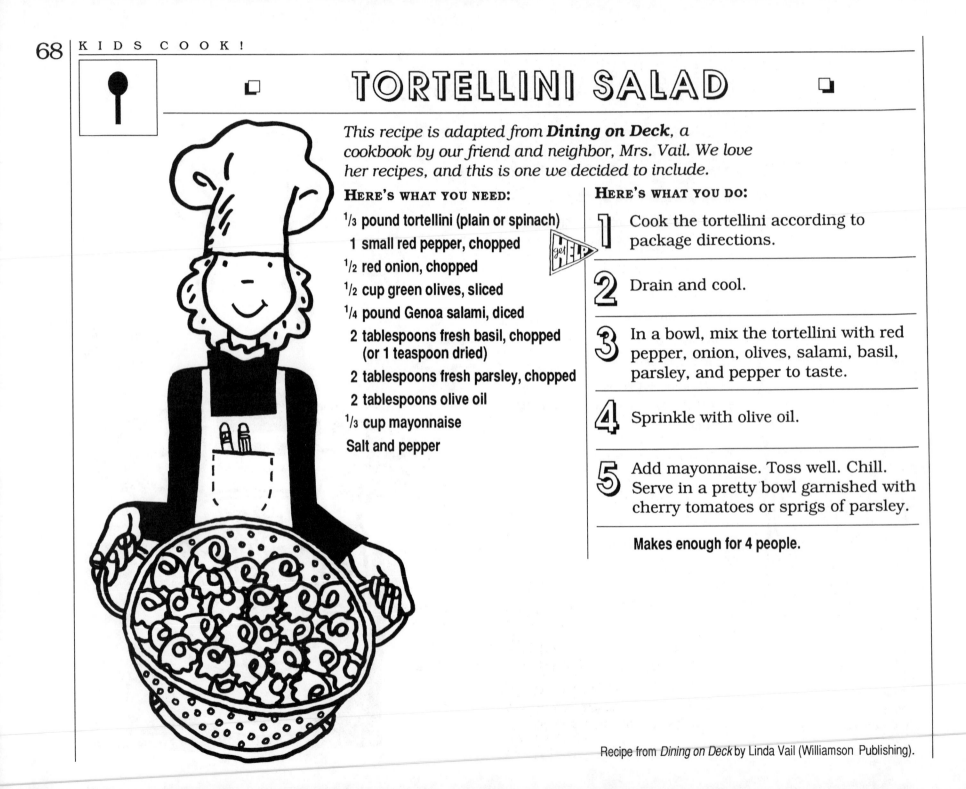

*This recipe is adapted from **Dining on Deck**, a cookbook by our friend and neighbor, Mrs. Vail. We love her recipes, and this is one we decided to include.*

HERE'S WHAT YOU NEED:

- ⅓ pound tortellini (plain or spinach)
- 1 small red pepper, chopped
- ½ red onion, chopped
- ½ cup green olives, sliced
- ¼ pound Genoa salami, diced
- 2 tablespoons fresh basil, chopped (or 1 teaspoon dried)
- 2 tablespoons fresh parsley, chopped
- 2 tablespoons olive oil
- ⅓ cup mayonnaise
- Salt and pepper

HERE'S WHAT YOU DO:

1. Cook the tortellini according to package directions.

2. Drain and cool.

3. In a bowl, mix the tortellini with red pepper, onion, olives, salami, basil, parsley, and pepper to taste.

4. Sprinkle with olive oil.

5. Add mayonnaise. Toss well. Chill. Serve in a pretty bowl garnished with cherry tomatoes or sprigs of parsley.

Makes enough for 4 people.

Recipe from *Dining on Deck* by Linda Vail (Williamson Publishing).

Eating seems to be a national pastime — especially among kids and teens. In fact, people tend to eat throughout the day, rather than just at mealtime. Snacking has become so popular that eating lots of light meals is now called "grazing." The truth is that snacking is fine as long as you don't fill up on empty, sugar-packed or fat-laden calories. Instead, try to snack on flavorful foods with some nutritional value. It's not that hard to do — just pick wisely and think about what you are putting into your body.

Side dishes are also more important than ever. They can really jazz up a ho-hum meal. Try some *Puffy Popovers* the next time you want a super snack or want to make a meal special. You'll see what we mean (they're great!). Look through this section of the book when you are home after school and are craving something good to eat and easy to prepare. You'll find a lot of good recipes to choose from.

NACHO NIBBLES

When we get tired of the usual snacks or when the whole family is craving something special, this is what we ask Zachary to make. It's one of his specialties!

HERE'S WHAT YOU NEED:

1 package of nacho chips

1 jar of salsa

Cheddar cheese (or your choice)

Green olives

NUTRI-NOTE

To keep healthy, be sure to eat at least four servings of fruits and vegetables every day, reduce your total fat intake, maintain adequate calcium intake, and balance the amount and kind of food you eat with physical activity to maintain a healthy body weight. Eating something like *Easy Summer Salsa* (see page 71) or *Great Gazpacho* (see page 42) for a snack shows you just how easy it is to meet your daily food requirements.

HERE'S WHAT YOU DO:

1 Cover a large microwave-safe plate with the nacho chips.

2 On every chip, put about 1 spoonful of salsa.

3 Cover the chips with lots of cheese (either sliced, or grated is fine).

4 Scatter a few olives on the cheese-covered chips.

5 Cook in the microwave on high or full power for 1 minute and 20 seconds, or until the cheese is melted.

6 Remove from the microwave carefully, as plate may be very hot.

Note: To cook in the oven, preheat to 350°. Place nacho chips on a pizza pan and follow recipe. Bake for about 10 minutes, or until cheese is bubbly.

Makes enough for 4 to 6 people.

EASY SUMMER SALSA

Although you can buy many different kinds of good salsa, in the summer when there are lots of fresh vegetables it is fun to make this. Serve it with chips or as a side dish with grilled meat or fish.

HERE'S WHAT YOU NEED:

1/2 cup tomatoes, diced

1/2 cup green peppers, diced

1/2 cup scallions or onions, chopped

1 tablespoon minced fresh garlic

1 tablespoon vinegar

1 tablespoon olive oil

HERE'S WHAT YOU DO:

1 Prepare all ingredients. Toss together. Refrigerate in a covered container until ready to serve. Experiment with different kinds of vinegar and additional vegetables like cucumbers and celery.

Makes 1 1/2 cups.

SARAH'S GUACAMOLE

*This is a delicious dip that can be served with nacho chips or fresh veggies. It is also good as a side dish with **Nacho Nibbles** and with **Famous Taco Salad**.*

Note: If you are not going to serve this immediately, cover the guacamole with a thin layer of mayonnaise or sour cream to keep it from turning brown. Keep refrigerated. Before serving, either scoop off this protective layer or mix it in.

HERE'S WHAT YOU NEED:

3 medium-sized ripe avocados, peeled and cubed

1 medium-sized tomato, diced

1 small onion, chopped finely

2 tablespoons lemon juice

1/2 teaspoon salt

1 drop tabasco

HERE'S WHAT YOU DO:

1 In a bowl, mash the avocados with a fork or potato masher.

2 Add the tomatoes and mix well.

3 Add the onion, lemon juice, salt, and tabasco.

4 Mix together and serve with your favorite nacho chips.

Makes 2 cups.

TORTILLA PIZZAS

You can buy whole wheat tortillas at the grocery store, usually in the section where they sell fresh pasta and cheeses. This is a delicious snack and also makes a nice appetizer or lunch.

HERE'S WHAT YOU NEED:

1 whole wheat tortilla

½ cup tomato or marinara sauce

½ cup chopped green pepper

½ cup chopped onion

Other pizza toppings of your choice

1 cup mozzarella cheese, shredded

HERE'S WHAT YOU DO:

1 Preheat oven to 400°.

2 Spray pizza pan or cookie sheet with no-stick spray.

3 Place tortilla on pan. Spread tomato sauce on top. Layer your other toppings on, one kind at a time (or in sections).

4 Sprinkle the cheese over all.

5 Bake at 400° for 5 minutes, until cheese melts.

Makes 1 pizza.

LAYERED TACO SPREAD

This is one of the most popular appetizer-type snacks that we make. Everyone from our youngest cousins to our grandparents likes this.

NUTRI·NOTE

How much sodium (salt) is in products labeled "low sodium"? Products labeled "low sodium" can contain no more than 140 mg. of sodium per serving. This is not to be confused with "sodium-free" products, which contain fewer than 5 mg.

HERE'S WHAT YOU NEED:

- 8 ounces cream cheese
- 8 ounces sour cream
- 1 jar (8 to 12 ounces) medium taco sauce
- 1 cup cheese, shredded, your choice
- 1/2 cup chopped tomato
- 1/2 cup chopped green pepper
- 1/2 cup black olives, sliced

HERE'S WHAT YOU DO:

1. Mix the cream cheese and sour cream until smooth. Pour it onto the bottom of a serving dish or pie dish.

2. Pour the taco sauce on top of the cream cheese mixture. Sprinkle half of the cheese on top.

3. Layer the vegetables on, one vegetable at a time.

4. Sprinkle the remaining cheese on top. Serve with nacho chips.

Makes enough for 8 people.

WAYNE & GARTH PARTY MIX

A great and easy way to give something good to eat to friends who come over to watch a movie, play a game, or sit around and talk.

HERE'S WHAT YOU NEED:

8 cups cereal (puffed corn, Crispix®, Wheat Chex®, or other similar cereal)

1 cup peanuts, shelled

1/2 cup melted butter or margarine

1/2 tablespoon Worcestershire sauce

2 drops tabasco

1 teaspoon celery salt

1/2 teaspoon onion salt

1/4 teaspoon garlic salt

HERE'S WHAT YOU DO:

1 Preheat oven to 250°.

2 Mix all of the ingredients together in a large bowl.

3 Pour into baking pan and bake at 250° for 1 hour, stirring occasionally.

4 Cool before serving. Store in airtight container.

Makes enough for a lot of friends.

do you know?

Acne isn't caused by eating pizza, potato chips, French fries, or chocolate. Most dermatologists believe that eating habits have little to do with "break outs." Acne is most often caused by the changing hormones in kids' bodies that naturally occurs as they get older. For some teens and adults, certain foods can aggravate the problem.

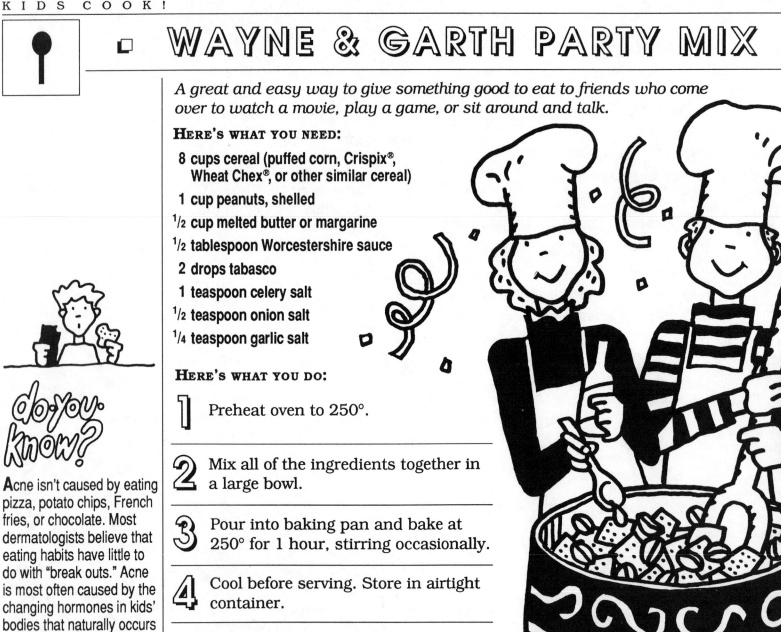

NO-COOK KABOBS

Skewer any of the following ingredients on a toothpick or skewer and serve to anyone. Try to come up with a colorful, appetizing combination. This is one of those good-tasting and good-for-you snacks.

Fruit	**Cheese**	**Cooked Meat**	**Vegetables**
Apples	Swiss	Chicken	Zucchini
Peaches	Muenster	Ham	Mushrooms
Pears	Mozzarella	Roast beef	Green or red
	Monterey	Turkey	pepper
	Gouda		Cucumber
	Edam		Celery
	Cheddar		Cauliflower
	American		Carrots
			Broccoli

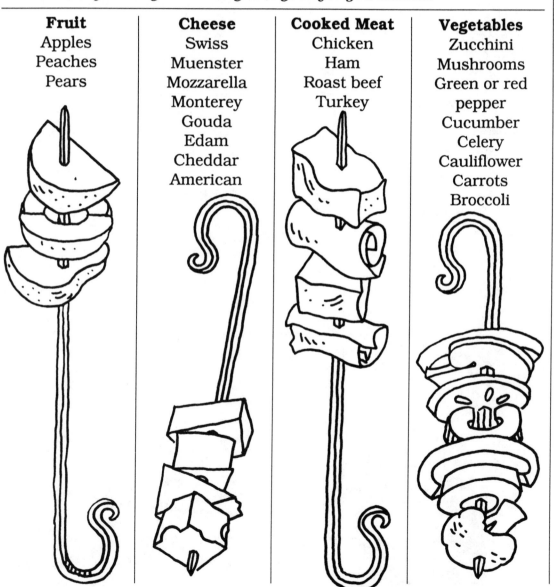

SAFETY ALERT!

Do you know how to do the Heimlich Maneuver? This is a simple procedure you can follow to save someone who is choking. If you do not know how to do it, ask your teacher to teach you or ask if your teacher will get a volunteer from your local emergency rescue squad to come to your class and teach you and your friends.

EGG BOATS

Stuffed eggs, deviled eggs — no matter what you call them, just about everyone loves them. We've called them **Egg Boats** *since our preschool days at the Red Balloon School.*

HERE'S WHAT YOU NEED:

5 eggs, hard-boiled

¼ cup mayonnaise

Paprika

Salt and pepper to taste

HERE'S WHAT YOU DO:

1 Prepare hard-boiled eggs (see page 50). Peel eggs carefully, being sure to remove all the shell.

2 Cut eggs in half lengthwise.

3 Put eggs yolks in a small bowl with the mayonnaise and mash with a fork. Add salt and pepper if you wish.

4 Refill egg whites with the yolk mixture.

5 Sprinkle with paprika and serve chilled.

Makes 10 egg boats.

Note: If you wish, try adding either ½ teaspoon Dijon-style mustard or ¼ teaspoon curry powder during step 4.

KiDS CAN!

William K. Chico Johnson was able to spin 81 hula hoops at one time. All of them spun between his shoulders and his hips.

ROASTED PUMPKIN SEEDS

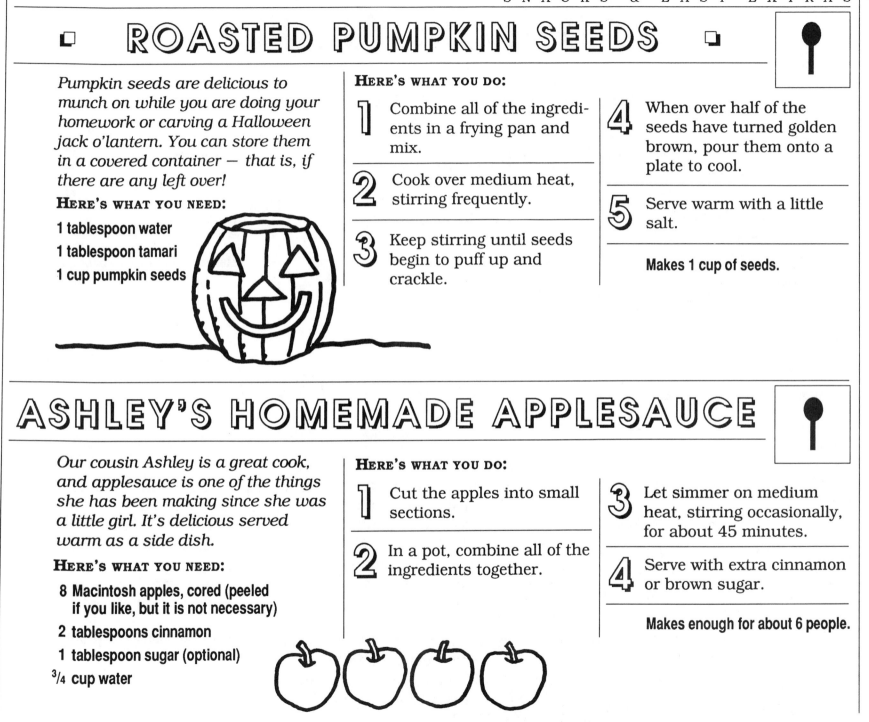

Pumpkin seeds are delicious to munch on while you are doing your homework or carving a Halloween jack o'lantern. You can store them in a covered container — that is, if there are any left over!

HERE'S WHAT YOU NEED:

1 tablespoon water

1 tablespoon tamari

1 cup pumpkin seeds

HERE'S WHAT YOU DO:

1 Combine all of the ingredients in a frying pan and mix.

2 Cook over medium heat, stirring frequently.

3 Keep stirring until seeds begin to puff up and crackle.

4 When over half of the seeds have turned golden brown, pour them onto a plate to cool.

5 Serve warm with a little salt.

Makes 1 cup of seeds.

ASHLEY'S HOMEMADE APPLESAUCE

Our cousin Ashley is a great cook, and applesauce is one of the things she has been making since she was a little girl. It's delicious served warm as a side dish.

HERE'S WHAT YOU NEED:

8 Macintosh apples, cored (peeled if you like, but it is not necessary)

2 tablespoons cinnamon

1 tablespoon sugar (optional)

3/4 cup water

HERE'S WHAT YOU DO:

1 Cut the apples into small sections.

2 In a pot, combine all of the ingredients together.

3 Let simmer on medium heat, stirring occasionally, for about 45 minutes.

4 Serve with extra cinnamon or brown sugar.

Makes enough for about 6 people.

HOT ARTICHOKE APPETIZER

This easy recipe tastes so good that everyone always thinks it is difficult to make. It makes a good appetizer, snack, or side dish.

HERE'S WHAT YOU NEED:

1 can of artichoke hearts, drained, chopped

1 cup mayonnaise

1 cup Parmesan cheese, grated

Dash of garlic powder

HERE'S WHAT YOU DO:

1 Preheat oven to 350°.

2 Mix all of the ingredients together.

3 Pour into a small baking dish.

4 Bake at 350° for 30 minutes, until bubbling.

5 Serve warm in the casserole dish with crackers or pita bread triangles for dipping.

Makes enough for 10 people.

SHRIMP SPREAD

If you like shrimp, you'll love this.

HERE'S WHAT YOU NEED:

1 package (8 ounces) cream cheese

2 tablespoons mayonnaise

1/2 teaspoon finely diced onion

1/2 teaspoon Worcestershire sauce

1 can any-sized shrimp (tiny shrimp are fine)

Dash of salt and pepper

1 tablespoon ketchup

1 teaspoon lemon juice

1 teaspoon horseradish

HERE'S WHAT YOU DO:

1 In a medium-sized bowl, cream together the cream cheese and mayonnaise. Add the onion, Worcestershire sauce, and salt and pepper. Set aside.

2 In a small bowl, mash the shrimp with a fork or potato masher. Add the ketchup, lemon juice, and horseradish, and mix well.

3 Add the shrimp to the cream cheese mixture and mix well. Serve in a pretty dish, garnished with parsley or cherry tomatoes. Serve chilled with crackers or wedges of pita bread.

Makes enough for 10 people.

BAKING POWDER BISCUITS

These are so good, especially if you come home from school feeling starved. When served warm with butter and jam, they can't be beat. They go well with most dinners, too. When reheated in the microwave, the leftovers are good for breakfast.

HERE'S WHAT YOU NEED:

1³/₄ cups all-purpose flour

3 teaspoons baking powder

¹/₂ teaspoon salt

5 tablespoons shortening

1 cup milk

HERE'S WHAT YOU DO:

1 Preheat oven to 450°.

2 Sift the flour, baking powder, and salt into a large bowl.

3 Cut-in the shortening by taking two dull knives (one in each hand) and literally cutting into the shortening, rather than mixing and mashing it. The batter should end up being crumbly.

4 Make a hole in the center of the dough and pour in the milk. Stir the dough for only a minute, trying to get the flour off the sides of the bowl.

5 Drop onto an ungreased cookie sheet or into lined muffin tins one teaspoonful at a time.

6 Bake at 450° for 12 to 15 minutes, or until golden brown.

7 Serve warm with butter and jam.

Makes about 20 small biscuits.

NUTRI-NOTE

There are a number of easy ways that kids can cut fat and cholesterol from foods. Here's how:

• Use the leanest chicken, red meat, or fish you can find. Cut away all visible fat from meat, and take the skin off chicken.

• When buying milk or milk products such as hard or soft cheeses, choose those which are low-fat (1 percent milk fat or skim). Limit egg consumption to 3 to 4 per week, or substitute two egg whites for one egg yolk.

• Instead of using butter or lard, choose vegetable oils such as safflower, corn, or canola oil, or use margarine.

PUFFY POPOVERS

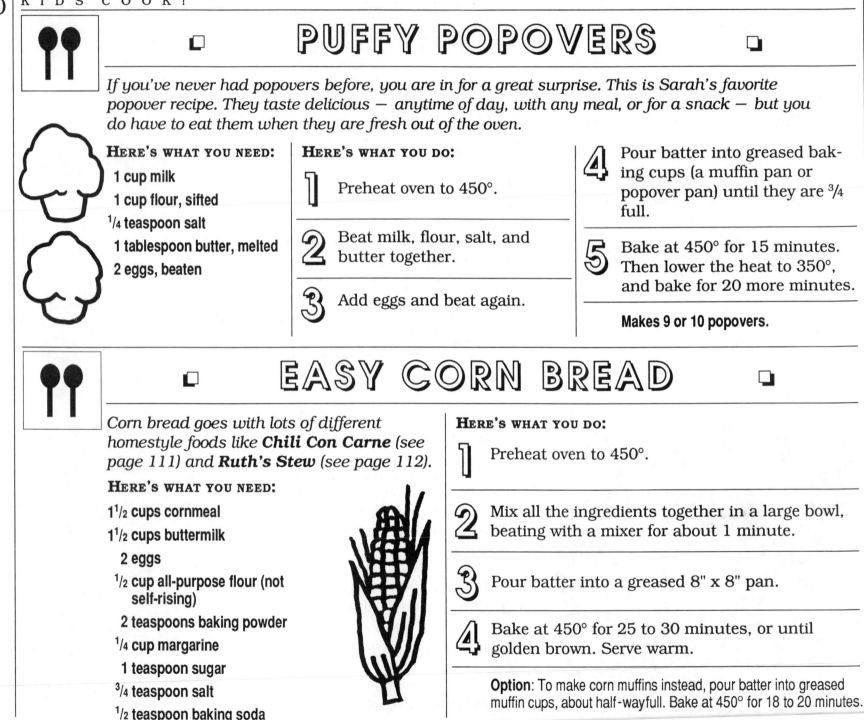

If you've never had popovers before, you are in for a great surprise. This is Sarah's favorite popover recipe. They taste delicious — anytime of day, with any meal, or for a snack — but you do have to eat them when they are fresh out of the oven.

HERE'S WHAT YOU NEED:

1 cup milk

1 cup flour, sifted

1/4 teaspoon salt

1 tablespoon butter, melted

2 eggs, beaten

HERE'S WHAT YOU DO:

1   Preheat oven to 450°.

2   Beat milk, flour, salt, and butter together.

3   Add eggs and beat again.

4   Pour batter into greased baking cups (a muffin pan or popover pan) until they are 3/4 full.

5   Bake at 450° for 15 minutes. Then lower the heat to 350°, and bake for 20 more minutes.

Makes 9 or 10 popovers.

EASY CORN BREAD

*Corn bread goes with lots of different homestyle foods like **Chili Con Carne** (see page 111) and **Ruth's Stew** (see page 112).*

HERE'S WHAT YOU NEED:

1 1/2 cups cornmeal

1 1/2 cups buttermilk

2 eggs

1/2 cup all-purpose flour (not self-rising)

2 teaspoons baking powder

1/4 cup margarine

1 teaspoon sugar

3/4 teaspoon salt

1/2 teaspoon baking soda

HERE'S WHAT YOU DO:

1   Preheat oven to 450°.

2   Mix all the ingredients together in a large bowl, beating with a mixer for about 1 minute.

3   Pour batter into a greased 8" x 8" pan.

4   Bake at 450° for 25 to 30 minutes, or until golden brown. Serve warm.

Option: To make corn muffins instead, pour batter into greased muffin cups, about half-way full. Bake at 450° for 18 to 20 minutes.

BANANA BREAD

We have so many recipes for banana bread that we didn't know which one to include, so one day Sarah baked six different kinds of banana bread and we had a taste test. This is the recipe we all liked best.

HERE'S WHAT YOU NEED:

1 egg

$2/3$ cup sour cream

$1/3$ cup honey

1 teaspoon vanilla extract

$1\frac{1}{2}$ cups ripe or overripe bananas, mashed

$2\frac{1}{4}$ cups flour

$1\frac{1}{2}$ teaspoons baking powder

1 teaspoon baking soda

$1/2$ teaspoon salt

$1/2$ teaspoon cinnamon

1 cup nuts (optional)

HERE'S WHAT YOU DO:

1 Preheat the oven to 350°.

2 In a large bowl, beat the egg until light colored.

3 Add the sour cream, honey, and vanilla, and beat again.

4 Mash the bananas with a potato masher or a fork. Add to the egg mixture, and combine well.

5 Add the nuts (optional).

6 Sift together the flour, baking powder, baking soda, cinnamon, and salt.

7 Combine with banana mixture, and blend lightly until mixed all the way through.

8 Place the batter in a greased $8\frac{1}{2}$" x $4\frac{1}{2}$" loaf pan.

9 Bake at 350° for about 1 hour, or until bread is browned. Cool before slicing.

Makes about 10 slices.

do you know?

June is dairy month. Try some milk shakes and new, lower fat cheeses this June. And every day, have the best snack of all — a nice, tall, cold glass of milk.

CAPE COD SPECIAL

Our dad taught Zachary how to make this tangy drink on Cape Cod, and now Zachary saves it to prepare only on special occasions.

HERE'S WHAT YOU NEED:

1 cup V8® or tomato juice, chilled

3 drops tabasco sauce

1/8 teaspoon Worcestershire sauce

1/2 teaspoon horseradish

1 lemon wedge

A stick of celery (optional)

HERE'S WHAT YOU DO:

1. In a large glass, combine all of the ingredients. Be sure that you only put in as much as the recipe calls for, because these ingredients are very spicy and could burn your mouth if you put too much of something in!

2. Mix well with a spoon.

3. Serve over ice, with a celery stick.

4. Drink slowly!

Makes 1 glassful.

Note: If this is too spicy, then use only a drop of tabasco and 1/4 teaspoon of horseradish.

BAKED POTATOES

Baked potatoes are one of those cozy foods. Some people like them for lunch, split in half and topped with sauteed vegetables and melted cheese. They taste great with just a sprinkle of salt, or, if you want to splurge, have them topped with butter, sour cream, and some bits of bacon.

HERE'S WHAT YOU NEED:

Baking potatoes, such as Idaho or russet

HERE'S WHAT YOU DO:

1. Preheat oven to 375°.

2. Scrub potatoes well with potato scrubbing brush.

3. Puncture about 4 holes in each potato with the tip of a sharp knife. This is very important as otherwise the steam can't escape and the potatoes may explode.

4. Place potatoes directly on oven rack and bake at 375° for one hour. Serve with butter, sour cream, or crumbled bacon.

Makes as many as you want.

JAMMED POTATO SKINS

We ordered these in restaurants a lot and then started making our own. Our friends love them. Keep the potato that you scoop out to make mashed potatoes.

HERE'S WHAT YOU NEED:

Potatoes for baking, Idaho or russet

Cheddar cheese

Bacon

Sour cream

HERE'S WHAT YOU DO:

1 Preheat oven to 375°.

2 Scrub potatoes and pierce with a fork several times. Bake in oven for 1 hour.

3 Remove from oven and cool until you can handle comfortably. Split potatoes in half lengthwise and scoop out most of the potato into a bowl. Set aside potato to use in mashed potatoes or other recipes. If potatoes are large, cut the skins in half again, horizontally.

4 Slice cheddar cheese or cut into chunks and layer into skins.

5 Cook bacon according to microwave instructions on page 46. Be sure to have an adult help you with the bacon. (If no one is home, skip the bacon.) Once bacon is cooled, crumble it and place on top of cheddar cheese.

6 Return jammed skins to the oven in a baking pan or cookie sheet and bake about 10 minutes, or until cheese is bubbling.

7 Serve skins with a bowl of sour cream and some salsa or guacamole, too.

Makes 2 to 4 skins per potato.

Note: To use up the leftover potatoes, simply mash them with a potato masher. Add margarine, a little milk, and some salt and pepper for some great home-style mashed potatoes.

FRENCH FRIES

This is a great way to enjoy homemade **French Fries** *without getting into the danger of working with hot oil.*

HERE'S WHAT YOU NEED:

4 large potatoes

1 tablespoon white vinegar

4 tablespoons (½ stick) margarine

¼ cup canola or vegetable oil

do you know?

Cooking oils have 120 calories per tablespoon while butter and margarine have only 100 calories per tablespoon. That's because butter and margarine are 15 percent water. Because oils do not contain water, the fat content in them is more concentrated, and therefore higher in calories.

HERE'S WHAT YOU DO:

1 Preheat oven to 400°. Scrub the potatoes .

2 Peel the potatoes (or leave them unpeeled if you prefer) and cut them into about ¼"-thick strips.

3 Mix vinegar and enough cold water to cover the potatoes in a large bowl. Be sure potatoes are completely covered with water or they will turn brown when exposed to the air. If you like vinegary potatoes, add a little more vinegar to the water, or sprinkle a little extra vinegar on your potatoes right before you bake them.

4 Drain potatoes thoroughly, pat them dry with a paper towel, and put in a big bowl.

5 Melt margarine in a microwave or a saucepan. Remove from the heat, add oil, and stir. Pour mixture carefully over the potatoes and toss until well coated. Place potatoes on a cookie sheet.

6 Bake the potatoes at 400° for 35 to 40 minutes until golden brown, turning them about halfway through baking time so they brown all over.

7 Carefully remove baking sheet from the oven and serve your French fries while still hot. Be sure that there is plenty of salt, vinegar, and ketchup, too.

Makes enough for 4 people.

PARMESAN POTATO PIE

This is good, easy to make, and a nice change from the usual potatoes.
For an easy but special dinner that you can make yourself, prepare these
potatoes with **Green Bean Casserole** *(see page 113) and grilled chicken.*

HERE'S WHAT YOU NEED:

1 stick margarine

1 cup Parmesan cheese

6 or 7 raw potatoes

HERE'S WHAT YOU DO:

1 Preheat oven to 350°.

2 Grease the bottom of a glass pie dish (9" or 10") with margarine.

3 Sprinkle with some of the Parmesan cheese.

4 Peel the potatoes and slice thinly. (To keep the potatoes from turning brown, place in a bowl of cold water, until ready to cook.)

5 Melt the margarine in a saucepan or in the microwave. Mix in the remaining Parmesan cheese.

6 Layer the potatoes and the cheese mixture in the pie dish.

7 Bake at 350° for 1 hour, or until bottom is browned.

8 Flip onto a plate and serve while still warm.

Makes enough for about 6 people.

TWICE-BAKED POTATOES

*For some reason, in our family, **Twice-Baked Potatoes** have always been part of special dinners — like our dad's birthday dinner — but they are easy enough to make without a special occasion.*

HERE'S WHAT YOU NEED:

4 **potatoes, washed and scrubbed**

$1/4$ **cup milk**

$1/2$ **cup margarine**

$1/4$ **teaspoon salt**

$1/4$ **teaspoon pepper**

Grated cheddar cheese

Paprika

HERE'S WHAT YOU DO:

1. Puncture potatoes with a fork. Bake the potatoes at 375° for 1 hour.

2. Cool until you can touch them. Cut in half lengthwise.

3. Scoop out the potato into a bowl, being very careful not to break the skin.

4. Mash the potatoes with the milk and the margarine. Use either a potato masher, or for really smooth potatoes, use an electric mixer.

5. Refill the skins with the potato mixture.

6. Sprinkle the cheese on top and then sprinkle on some paprika.

7. Bake again at 350° for about 20 minutes or until heated through and the cheese is melted.

8. Serve hot.

Makes 8 potato halves.

SAFETY ALERT!

Turn pot handles inward so young children can't pull pots off the stove.

For years, ice cream shops have been popular detours on family outings. In fact, just about everyone has a favorite soda fountain treat, favorite flavor of ice cream, and even a favorite brand of gourmet ice cream!

In our family, we all fancy ourselves to be ice cream connoisseurs. Whenever we are away, we make it a point to try out the local ice cream shops and popular ice cream brands. Needless to say, we've incorporated a lot of special treats in this book from those we've sampled far and wide.

The good news is that you can concoct the soda fountain treat of your dreams right in your own kitchen. These recipes are for treats that are definitely good to the very last drop!

□ BEN & JERRY'S HOMEMADE™ □ SWEET CREAM ICE CREAM BASE

do·you· know?

July is ice cream month. Ice cream probably evolved from chilled wines and other iced drinks during the time of Alexander the Great. He loved iced foods. In the 1700s, ice cream was introduced to Americans. In 1818, Dolly Madison served ice cream to the guests at the Second Inaugural Ball at the White House.

With Vermont (where we live) the home of Ben & Jerry's Homemade™ Ice Cream, we are lucky to have delicious ice cream very often. Sometimes, though, we like to make our own, mixing in whatever we happen to have around the house to transform this sweet cream base into something very special. We make our ice cream in one of those newer freezers, so it only takes about five minutes of mixing, but you can use this recipe in whatever kind of ice cream freezer you have. Just follow the directions on your freezer.

HERE'S WHAT YOU NEED:

2 cups heavy or whipping cream

³/₄ cup sugar

²/₃ cup half-and-half

2 teaspoons vanilla extract (optional)

HERE'S WHAT YOU DO:

1 Pour the cream into a mixing bowl. Whisk in the sugar, a little at a time; then continue whisking until completely blended, about 1 minute more.

2 Pour in the half-and-half and whisk to blend. (Add 2 teaspoons vanilla extract if you want your base to have a vanilla flavor.)

3 Follow the instructions on your ice cream maker for further directions on making ice cream.

4 Scoop and serve plain, on top of brownies, or apple pie. You may also add mix-ins before the final freeze, such as any type of candy (M&M's® or a Heathbar®), cookies, or fruit (strawberries, peaches, or blueberries).

Makes enough for about 6 people.

Recipe from *Ben & Jerry's Homemade™ Ice Cream Book* (Workman Publishing).

MIX-INS & TOPPINGS

Some people like to mix extras into their ice cream, while others prefer them sprinkled over the top. If you prefer mix-ins, you can add them right near the end of the freeze of your homemade ice cream. If you are using storebought ice cream, mix it in by placing a scoop of ice cream on a cutting board. Mash it down with the back of a spoon, add the mix-in, and mash again. Then scoop into your dish. That's how they do it at the big scoop shops. Here are some of the many, many possible mix-ins.

Chocolate chips

Heathbars™, broken in pieces

M & M's™

Cookies, any kind

Reese's™ Peanut Butter Cups

Raisins

Coconut, shredded

Chocolate sprinkles

Fresh fruit, sliced

Gorp

Nuts, chopped, any kind

Peppermint stick candies

Granola

Chocolate bars, broken

Hot applesauce (topping only)

Hot maple syrup (topping only)

do you know?

A 12-ounce can of Coca-Cola™ contains NINE teaspoons of refined sugar and 26 mg. of caffeine. No wonder you couldn't sleep after drinking that can of soda!

STRAWBERRY PARFAIT

This is an easy-to-make dessert that can be very fancy. Ask if you can use some elegant parfait glasses or goblets to prepare this. If the glasses are on a long stem, always hold on to the stem while you are filling the glasses.

HERE'S WHAT YOU NEED:

Vanilla ice cream or lemon ice

***Fresh Strawberry Topping** (see page 99)*

***Homemade Whipped Cream** (see page 97)*

Note: You can make this ahead of time if you are planning a special surprise for someone. First, ask if you can put the special glasses in the freezer. If you can, then fill the glasses and return to the freezer for a few hours until you are ready to serve. Add the whipped cream and strawberry garnish right before you serve your parfaits.

HERE'S WHAT YOU DO:

1 Layer small amounts of ice cream and strawberries in a tall glass, so that you have stripes of color.

2 Top with a dollop of whipped cream and garnish with a whole strawberry, if you have any.

Makes as many as you want.

do you know?

Milk is one of the safest foods you can eat. In 1856, Dr. Louis Pasteur discovered that heat killed the germs in milk. Today your milk is "pasteurized" (heated). That makes it super safe to drink.

LOLLAPALOOZA

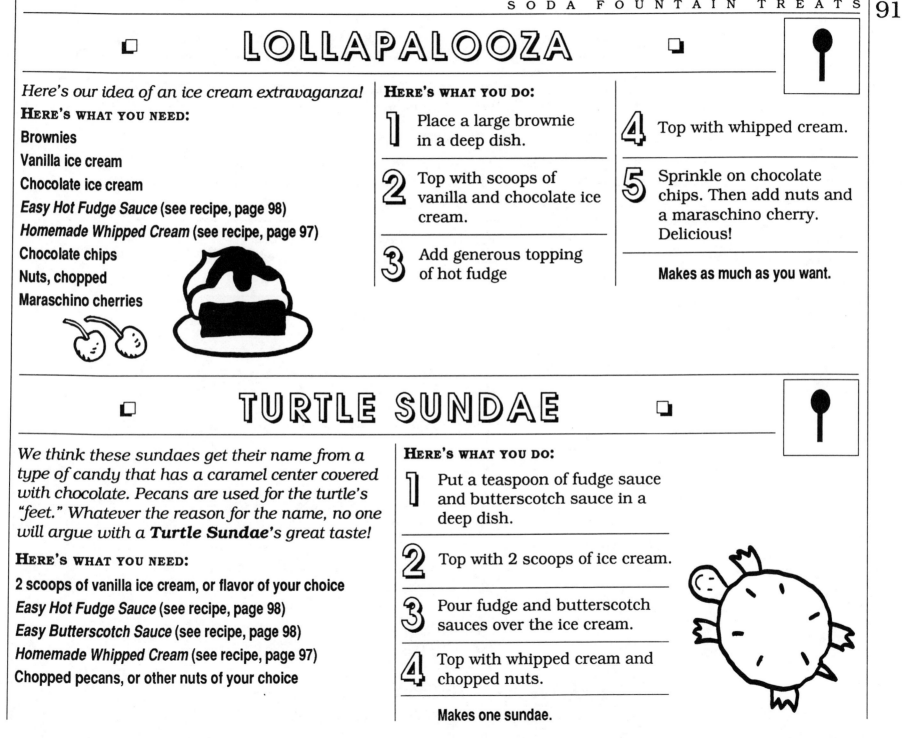

Here's our idea of an ice cream extravaganza!

HERE'S WHAT YOU NEED:

Brownies

Vanilla ice cream

Chocolate ice cream

Easy Hot Fudge Sauce **(see recipe, page 98)**

Homemade Whipped Cream **(see recipe, page 97)**

Chocolate chips

Nuts, chopped

Maraschino cherries

HERE'S WHAT YOU DO:

1 Place a large brownie in a deep dish.

2 Top with scoops of vanilla and chocolate ice cream.

3 Add generous topping of hot fudge

4 Top with whipped cream.

5 Sprinkle on chocolate chips. Then add nuts and a maraschino cherry. Delicious!

Makes as much as you want.

TURTLE SUNDAE

We think these sundaes get their name from a type of candy that has a caramel center covered with chocolate. Pecans are used for the turtle's "feet." Whatever the reason for the name, no one will argue with a **Turtle Sundae***'s great taste!*

HERE'S WHAT YOU NEED:

2 scoops of vanilla ice cream, or flavor of your choice

Easy Hot Fudge Sauce **(see recipe, page 98)**

Easy Butterscotch Sauce **(see recipe, page 98)**

Homemade Whipped Cream **(see recipe, page 97)**

Chopped pecans, or other nuts of your choice

HERE'S WHAT YOU DO:

1 Put a teaspoon of fudge sauce and butterscotch sauce in a deep dish.

2 Top with 2 scoops of ice cream.

3 Pour fudge and butterscotch sauces over the ice cream.

4 Top with whipped cream and chopped nuts.

Makes one sundae.

ICE CREAM COOKIE SANDWICH

Sarah makes this all the time. The next time you bake chocolate chip cookies, be sure to bake some a little larger than usual to use with this favorite after school treat!

HERE'S WHAT YOU NEED:

2 chocolate chip cookies, or other cookies of your choice

1 scoop of vanilla ice cream, or other ice cream of your choice

HERE'S WHAT YOU DO:

1 Place scoop of ice cream on bottom side of one cookie. Press ice cream flat with the back of spoon.

2 Top off with the other cookie, bottom side on the ice cream. Enjoy your ice cream sandwich.

Makes one ice cream sandwich.

CHOCOLATE MILK SHAKE

Zach makes this drink for Sarah when she's not feeling quite on top of the world.

HERE'S WHAT YOU NEED:

4 scoops of vanilla ice cream

3/4 cup milk

1/4 cup chocolate syrup

HERE'S WHAT YOU DO:

1 In a blender, combine all of the ingredients.

2 Blend on medium speed for about 15 seconds.

3 Serve with an additional scoop of ice cream floating in each glass.

Makes 2 glasses.

CHOCOLATE ICE CREAM SODA

Here's another very easy, very quick, and delicious ice cream treat.

HERE'S WHAT YOU NEED:

Chocolate syrup

1/2 cup milk

Vanilla or chocolate ice cream

Seltzer or club soda

HERE'S WHAT YOU DO:

1 Pour some chocolate syrup into bottom of a large glass (about 3 tablespoons or to suit your taste).

2 Add milk and stir until well mixed.

3 Add enough seltzer to fill large glass to halfway. Then scoop in ice cream, and add seltzer to fill to top of glass.

4 Serve with a straw and a spoon.

Makes one ice cream soda.

do you know?

What's the difference between a frappe, a milk shake, a thick shake, a float, and an ice cream soda? Well, in some parts of the country, these names are interchangeable, but here is what these terms mean to us.

A *frappe* or *thick shake* is made in a blender with a lot of ice cream and a little milk, plus a flavored syrup.

A *milk shake* is made in a blender with a lot of milk, a flavored syrup, and, sometimes, a scoop of ice cream. They are all blended together.

A *float* is usually made with a flavored soda, such as root beer, and scoops of ice cream "floating" in the soda, but not blended in.

An *ice cream soda* is usually made with milk, seltzer, and a flavored syrup. It is topped off with ice cream that is not blended in.

Now, do you know the difference between a sundae and a parfait? Well, to us they are almost the same, except that parfaits are served in restaurants in tall, thin glasses that are fancier than sundae dishes. Also, parfaits have pretty layers of a little ice cream and sauce, repeated over and over. Sundaes usually have sauce on the bottom, lots of ice cream, and then sauce on top, and they are bigger and messier.

ROOT BEER FLOAT

This is probably the quickest and easiest soda fountain treat, and it is scrumptious. Try one!

HERE'S WHAT YOU NEED:

Root beer soda

Vanilla ice cream

Option: This can be made with any kind of soda. A "Brown Cow" is a float made with a cola and vanilla ice cream. It's also very good made with raspberry soda or with 7-UP™.

HERE'S WHAT YOU DO:

1 Put two scoops of ice cream in a tall glass.

2 Slowly add root beer soda, so that the glass doesn't fill up with foam. Stir ever-so-slightly so flavors begin to mix.

Makes one float.

ZACH'S ROOT BEER FRAPPE

This is a cross between a root beer float and a milk shake. It's one of our favorite concoctions.

HERE'S WHAT YOU NEED:

5 scoops vanilla ice cream

$3/4$ cup milk

$1/2$ cup root beer soda

$1/2$ teaspoon vanilla extract

$1/8$ teaspoon confectioners' sugar

HERE'S WHAT YOU DO:

1 Combine all of the ingredients in a blender, using only three scoops of the vanilla ice cream.

2 Blend for about 3 seconds.

3 Serve in tall glasses with large scoops of ice cream floating on top.

Makes 2 glasses.

STRAWBERRY ICE

This is easy to make, yet it looks and tastes like a gourmet dessert. It is very light and is good on a hot summer's day. If you don't have an ice cream maker, you can still make this, but plan ahead, because you have to let it set in the freezer for a long time (see recipe).

HERE'S WHAT YOU NEED:

³/₄ cup sugar

¹/₂ cup water

3 cups fresh strawberries, hulled

¹/₄ cup lime juice

¹/₄ cup orange juice

SAFETY ALERT!

Water and electricity can cause serious shocks so make sure that your hands are dry before using electrical appliances. Always unplug appliances when not in use. Never come in contact with water when around electrical appliances. If you drop an appliance in the water while it is plugged in, don't reach in to take it out. If an appliance gets wet, make sure to have it serviced before you use it again.

HERE'S WHAT YOU DO:

1 In a small saucepan, combine the water and the sugar. Bring to a boil, stirring constantly to prevent burning. (You may want an adult to help with this, as sugar burns easily.) *get help*

2 Remove from the heat and put in refrigerator to cool.

3 Put the remaining ingredients in the blender, and blend until smooth, only about 5 seconds.

4 Once the sugar mixture has cooled (about 15 minutes), mix it in with the strawberry mixture.

With an ice cream maker:
Follow the directions of the ice cream maker.

Without an ice cream maker:

5 Cover and freeze the mixture for 4 to 5 hours or until almost firm.

6 Transfer the mixture into a bowl.

7 Beat with an electric beater on medium speed for 2 minutes or until fluffy.

8 Cover and freeze for another 6 hours or until firm.

Makes enough for 7 people.

ORANGE CREAMSICLE

A delicious treat for either a hot day or a rainy day. It makes a great snack during a T.V. baseball or football game!

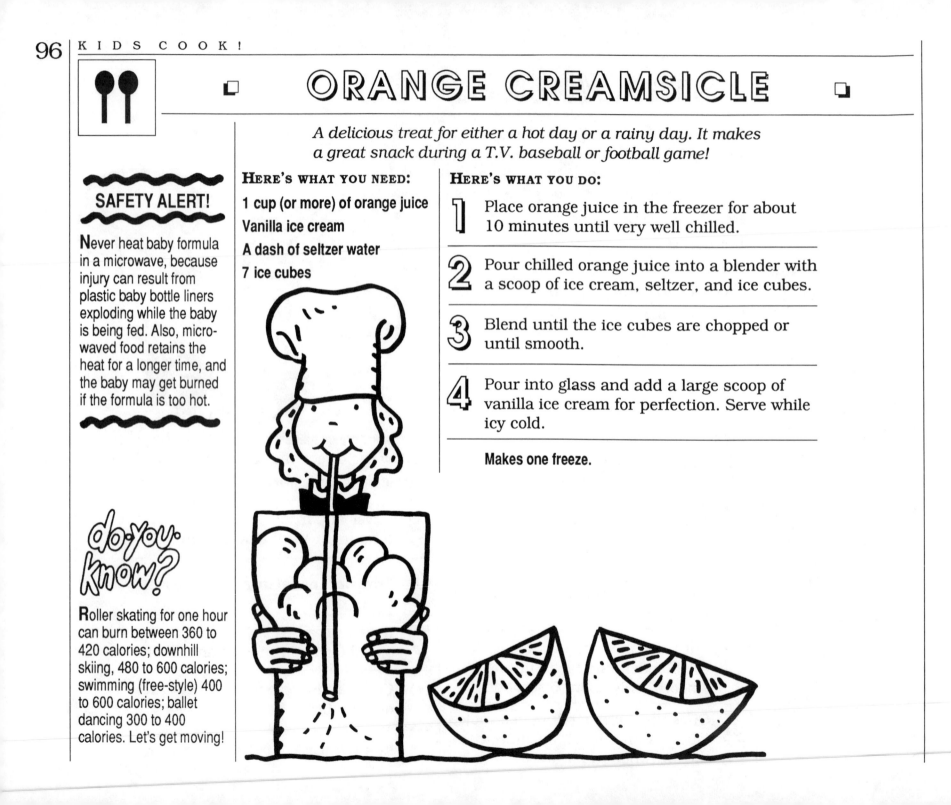

SAFETY ALERT!

Never heat baby formula in a microwave, because injury can result from plastic baby bottle liners exploding while the baby is being fed. Also, micro-waved food retains the heat for a longer time, and the baby may get burned if the formula is too hot.

do you know?

Roller skating for one hour can burn between 360 to 420 calories; downhill skiing, 480 to 600 calories; swimming (free-style) 400 to 600 calories; ballet dancing 300 to 400 calories. Let's get moving!

HERE'S WHAT YOU NEED:

1 cup (or more) of orange juice

Vanilla ice cream

A dash of seltzer water

7 ice cubes

HERE'S WHAT YOU DO:

1 Place orange juice in the freezer for about 10 minutes until very well chilled.

2 Pour chilled orange juice into a blender with a scoop of ice cream, seltzer, and ice cubes.

3 Blend until the ice cubes are chopped or until smooth.

4 Pour into glass and add a large scoop of vanilla ice cream for perfection. Serve while icy cold.

Makes one freeze.

PEACH COOLER

If you like peaches, this is a terrific way to enjoy them.

HERE'S WHAT YOU NEED:

1 cup milk

1 cup fresh peaches, peeled and sliced (You can use canned peaches packed in own juices and drained.)

2 or 3 drops of almond extract

1 cup vanilla ice cream

Dash of salt

HERE'S WHAT YOU DO:

1 In a blender, combine all of the ingredients, except the ice cream.

2 Cover and blend at about medium speed (liquify speed, if you have it) until smooth.

3 Stop blender and add the ice cream.

4 Blend the mixture again at low speed (blend speed, if you have it).

Makes about 2 glasses.

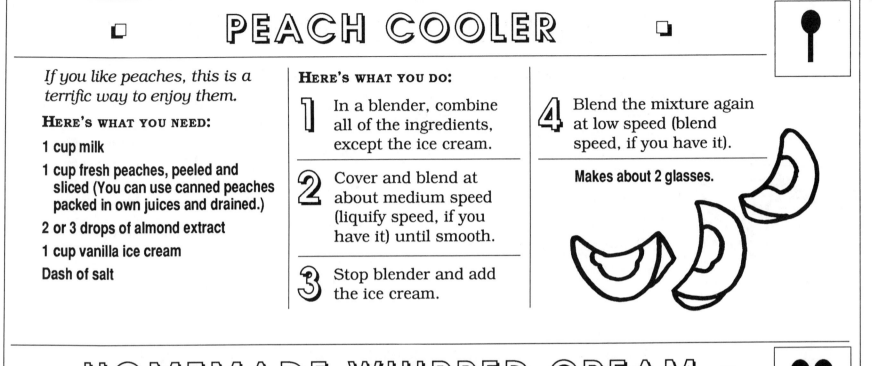

HOMEMADE WHIPPED CREAM

*A delicious topping for any kind of a dessert, **Homemade Whipped Cream** is much better than storebought. After you make it a few times, you will get a feeling for when it is done.*

HERE'S WHAT YOU NEED:

1 pint whipping cream

3 tablespoons confectioners' sugar

1 teaspoon vanilla extract

HERE'S WHAT YOU DO:

1 Put the tongs of the beater and a metal bowl in the freezer at least 20 minutes before use. Be sure whipping cream is cold, too.

2 Pour all the ingredients in the chilled bowl, and beat on high speed until soft peaks begin to form.

3 Whipped cream is done when soft peaks form and it starts to get stiffer. Store in refrigerator until ready to use.

Makes enough to top 8 to 10 desserts.

EASY BUTTERSCOTCH SAUCE

This butterscotch sauce served hot on coffee ice cream is one of our mom's favorite treats. This is an easy sauce to make and you can serve it warm or cold. For another kind of butterscotch sauce, see page 152.

HERE'S WHAT YOU NEED:

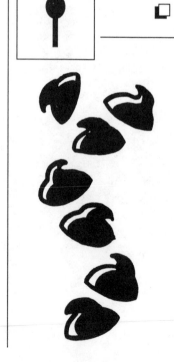

3 tablespoons margarine

½ cup brown sugar (light or dark)

¼ cup heavy cream or evaporated milk

HERE'S WHAT YOU DO:

1 Combine all ingredients in a small saucepan. Simmer for 5 minutes.

2 Pour into bowl and beat for about 30 seconds.

3 Serve hot or cold on ice cream.

Makes enough for 3 sundaes.

EASY HOT FUDGE SAUCE

Here's a very easy hot fudge sauce that we make very often.

HERE'S WHAT YOU NEED:

1 package (12 ounces) chocolate chips

1 can (12 ounces) evaporated milk

1 cup sugar

1 tablespoon margarine

1 teaspoon vanilla extract

HERE'S WHAT YOU DO:

1 Combine chocolate chips, evaporated milk and sugar in a medium saucepan.

2 Bring to a boil over medium heat, stirring constantly. *(get HELP)*

3 Remove from heat and add margarine and vanilla extract.

4 Serve warm or cold, and store any extra sauce in the refrigerator.

Makes about 2½ cups of sauce.

FRESH STRAWBERRY TOPPING

Slicing up fresh strawberries into a wonderful topping is about the best thing you can do for a bowl of vanilla ice cream or a piece of plain cake. Our dad loves this on his cereal, too. And don't forget pancakes, waffles, or French toast!

HERE'S WHAT YOU NEED:

- 1 pint of fresh strawberries, hulled and sliced
- 2 tablespoons sugar (more or less, depending on how sweet the berries are)

HERE'S WHAT YOU DO:

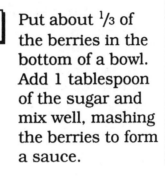

1 Put about ⅓ of the berries in the bottom of a bowl. Add 1 tablespoon of the sugar and mix well, mashing the berries to form a sauce.

2 Add the remaining berries (don't mash these) and sugar. Gently mix through. Refrigerate until using.

Makes 1 pint of topping.

VERY BERRY SAUCE

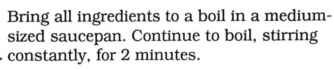

You can make this with frozen strawberries or raspberries. Either way it makes a wonderful sauce for ice cream sundaes, pancakes, or waffles.

HERE'S WHAT YOU NEED:

- 1 package (10 ounces) frozen and thawed sweetened berries
- ½ teaspoon cornstarch
- 1 tablespoon light corn syrup

HERE'S WHAT YOU DO:

1 Bring all ingredients to a boil in a medium-sized saucepan. Continue to boil, stirring constantly, for 2 minutes.

2 Remove pan from heat and cool.

3 Pour into covered container and refrigerate. The sauce will get thicker as it cools. Pour over your favorite ice cream.

Makes about 1 cup of sauce.

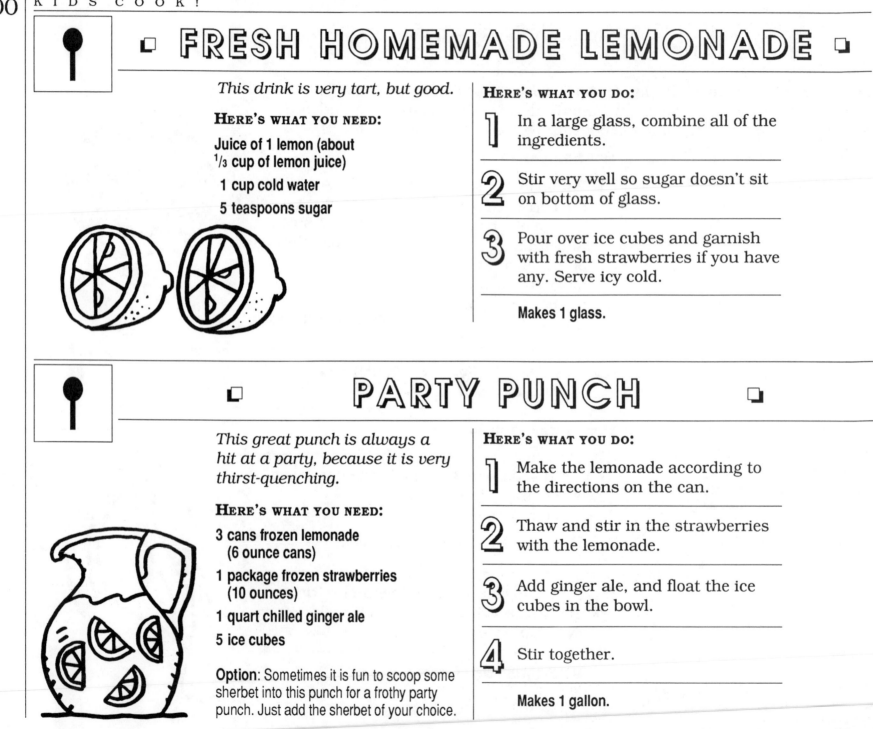

FRESH HOMEMADE LEMONADE

This drink is very tart, but good.

HERE'S WHAT YOU NEED:

Juice of 1 lemon (about
$^{1}/_{3}$ cup of lemon juice)

1 cup cold water

5 teaspoons sugar

HERE'S WHAT YOU DO:

1. In a large glass, combine all of the ingredients.

2. Stir very well so sugar doesn't sit on bottom of glass.

3. Pour over ice cubes and garnish with fresh strawberries if you have any. Serve icy cold.

Makes 1 glass.

PARTY PUNCH

This great punch is always a hit at a party, because it is very thirst-quenching.

HERE'S WHAT YOU NEED:

3 cans frozen lemonade
(6 ounce cans)

1 package frozen strawberries
(10 ounces)

1 quart chilled ginger ale

5 ice cubes

Option: Sometimes it is fun to scoop some sherbet into this punch for a frothy party punch. Just add the sherbet of your choice.

HERE'S WHAT YOU DO:

1. Make the lemonade according to the directions on the can.

2. Thaw and stir in the strawberries with the lemonade.

3. Add ginger ale, and float the ice cubes in the bowl.

4. Stir together.

Makes 1 gallon.

DELICIOUS DINNERS

Learning how to help with your family's dinner can make a big difference in everyone's evening. In a lot of families, kids are just getting home from after-school activities, parents are getting home after a long day at work, and younger sisters and brothers may just be getting home from day care. Everyone is tired and hungry.

If you get home first and if you are allowed to cook without an adult at home, you can actually get dinner started. If you are not allowed to cook alone, then you can perhaps start preparing a salad or the batter for some biscuits, or set the table. You will be amazed at what a difference it will make in the rest of the evening for everyone, if you show some interest in helping with dinner.

If you are a beginning cook, there are still many recipes you can make. Try *Easy Green Bean Casserole*. You'll be surprised at how quickly you will progress to the point where you can prepare the main course! Want to make a special evening out of an ordinary week night? Set the table with cloth napkins or put a tiny vase with wildflowers or pretty leaves on the table. It's like magic!

TACOS

*When you're tired of hamburgers, here is a simple and creative meal using hamburger meat. We make **Tacos** a lot. It's a delicious lunch, too.*

do·you·know?

Salmonella poisoning can stem from many hidden sources. When grilling or barbecuing meat of any kind, be sure it is transferred onto a clean plate after cooking — not back onto the plate it was on when it was raw. Also, when using a marinade, make sure that you baste any meat long before you take it off the grill. Bacteria from the raw meat remains in the juices which spoil quickly, especially on hot summer days!

The latest cause of salmonella poisoning is raw eggs. Don't lick spoons of batter that contains raw eggs — even favorites like raw chocolate chip cookie dough and brownies are off limits now!

HERE'S WHAT YOU NEED:

1 pound hamburger

8 ounces taco or tomato sauce

Taco shells

Cheese, grated or diced, your choice

Lettuce, washed, dried, and shredded

Black olives, halved

Tomatoes, diced

Onion, diced

Salsa

HERE'S WHAT YOU DO:

1 In a large frying pan, brown the hamburger with a little salt and pepper. Remove excess fat.

2 Once browned, add the tomato or taco sauce.

3 Heat through on medium heat.

4 Put taco shells in the oven at 250° for about 5 minutes, or until the shells are warmed and a little bit flexible.

5 Put the hamburger in the shells, then layer on the rest of the toppings, ending with the cheese. Serve with bowls of salsa, sour cream, and if you have time, *Sarah's Guacamole* (see page 71).

6 For baked tacos, put filled tacos in the oven (350°) and bake just until cheese is slightly melted, about 5 minutes.

Makes about 6 tacos.

STUFFED PEPPERS

Choosing different kinds of cooking oils can make a BIG difference in the amount and kind of fat you eat. Try to never use palm or coconut oil which is very high in saturated fat. Instead, choose canola oil, safflower oil, or vegetable oil.

HERE'S WHAT YOU NEED:

3 green peppers, washed, cut in half, lengthwise, and cleaned

Spaghetti sauce

1 — 2 — 3 Meatballs recipe, (see page 104)

Shredded cheese, optional

½ **cup bread crumbs mixed with 1 table-spoon melted margarine (optional)**

HERE'S WHAT YOU DO:

1 Preheat oven to 350°.

2 Follow the directions to prepare the meatballs (see page 104).

3 In a medium saucepan, bring enough water to cover the green peppers to a boil. Boil the peppers for about 3 minutes or until slightly softened. Drain and let cool.

4 Fill the green peppers with the meatball recipe.

5 Pour some spaghetti sauce into the bottom of a greased baking dish.

6 Place the green peppers in the sauce (pepper side down) and pour more sauce over the tops of the peppers. Sprinkle some grated cheese or buttered bread crumbs over the top of the peppers, if you wish.

7 Bake at 350° for 30 to 35 minutes .

Makes 6 stuffed peppers.

QUICK SPAGHETTI SAUCE WITH 1 — 2 — 3 MEATBALLS

Sarah serves this with a tossed salad and some fresh Italian bread for one of our favorite "kid-cooked" meals.

HERE'S WHAT YOU NEED:

Quick Spaghetti Sauce:

- 1 jar (30 ounces) spaghetti sauce
- 1 onion, chopped
- 1 clove garlic, minced
- 1½ tablespoons dried parsley
- 1 teaspoon oregano
- 1 to 2 tablespoons olive oil

Spaghetti

1 — 2 — 3 Meatballs, (see next page)

HERE'S WHAT YOU DO:

1 To make sauce, brown garlic and onions in oil, in a skillet.

2 Add spaghetti sauce, parsley, and oregano. Let simmer over low heat.

3 To make meatballs, see *1 — 2 — 3 Meatballs* recipe on next page.

4 Add meatballs to sauce and cook on medium heat until meatballs are cooked thoroughly, about 20 minutes. Stir through occasionally so sauce doesn't burn on bottom of pan.

get HELP

5 Cook spaghetti according to directions on package. Drain thoroughly.

6 Serve spaghetti with meatballs and sauce.

Makes enough for 6 people.

SAFETY ALERT!

If a child is cut, stop the bleeding by elevating the cut and applying gentle pressure with a clean cloth. Wash the wound and apply a bandage. If the bleeding is severe, continue to elevate and apply pressure, and call for emergency help.

THE 1 — 2 — 3 MEATBALL RECIPE

HERE'S WHAT YOU NEED:

1 pound hamburger meat

2 eggs, beaten

$1/4$ cup water

$1/2$ cup bread crumbs

Salt and pepper to taste

HERE'S WHAT YOU DO:

1 Mix all of the ingredients together, using your hands.

2 Shape into meatballs.

3 Cook in sauce for about 20 minutes or follow stuffed pepper directions.

Makes about 10 meatballs.

Note: This recipe works for any meatball or stuffed pepper recipe.

STUFFED BURGERS

When hamburgers are on the menu, treat yourself to this surprise filling — or any filling you might like.

Special Occasions

Father's Day Barbecue

What do you do that is special for your dad on Father's Day? We always prepare a special dinner — usually a barbecue. Our dad always seems to be very pleased and proud of whatever we prepare. Here is a sample menu you might plan on using next Father's Day.

*Stuffed Burgers**

*Best Potato Salad**

Sliced tomatoes, lettuce, and onion

Pickles and olives

*Strawberry Shortcake with Homemade Whipped Cream**

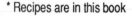

* Recipes are in this book

HERE'S WHAT YOU NEED:

Hamburger meat

Cream cheese

Margarine

Salt and pepper

HERE'S WHAT YOU DO:

1 Season hamburger meat with salt and pepper. Make two very thin hamburger patties.

2 Take a thin slice of cream cheese and put in the middle of one of the patties.

3 Lay the other patty on top, then pinch the edges together.

4 Grill on your barbecue. To pan fry, melt some margarine in a small frying pan. Cook the hamburger about 5 minutes on each side on medium heat, or until it is done the way you like.

5 Serve on a hamburger roll topped with lettuce, tomato, and all the other burger toppings you like.

Makes 1 stuffed hamburger.

Options: Try stuffing burgers with blue cheese, cheddar, salsa, red pepper relish, sliced pickles, or sauteed onions.

ZACH'S HOT DOGS WITH THE WORKS

Zachary makes this on Saturday nights when there is nothing that he likes to eat around the house.

HERE'S WHAT YOU NEED:

Hot dogs, with a slice down the middle, lengthwise

Margarine

Pillsbury® crescent rolls

Onion

Cheese

HERE'S WHAT YOU DO:

1. In a small frying pan, brown the hot dogs and a few thick slices of onion in margarine. Don't cook the hot dogs entirely; only cook for about 2 minutes.

2. Remove the hot dogs from the pan. Let the onions cook until golden brown.

3. When onions are done, place them in the slice down the middle of the hot dogs. Make sure that you don't burn your hands!

4. Lay 2 to 3 slices of cheese on top of the onions.

5. Wrap each hot dog entirely in crescent roll dough.

6. Place on a baking sheet, and bake in the oven at 350° for about 8 to 10 minutes, until crescent rolls are brown and cheese is melted.

Makes as many hot dogs as you want.

SLOPPY JOES

*Although **Sloppy Joes** are usually served on hamburger rolls, if you don't like soggy rolls, then serve this over flat egg noodles (follow package directions).*

HERE'S WHAT YOU NEED:

1 pound hamburger meat

1 large onion, chopped

1 clove garlic, minced

1 large green pepper, sliced lengthwise

1 jar (30 ounces) spaghetti sauce

Hamburger rolls

HERE'S WHAT YOU DO:

1 Brown the beef in a large frying pan.

2 Remove any excess grease.

3 Add the onion, garlic, peppers, and the spaghetti sauce.

4 Cover and let simmer on medium heat for about 45 minutes.

5 Serve over toasted hamburger rolls.

Makes enough for 6 people.

PIZZA ORIGINALE

It seems everyone has a favorite pizza place and a favorite pizza topping. We love the specialty pizzas at the Tucker Hill Lodge in Warren, Vermont. While our pizza that we make at home doesn't bear any resemblance to their gourmet pizzas, we did learn to expand our thinking about what you can put on pizza after tasting the wonderful flatbread pizzas they make in their stone ovens.

HERE'S WHAT YOU NEED:

1 pizza crust from the grocery store (look in the fresh pasta or dairy case for fresh pizza dough already shaped)

1 jar pizza, tomato, or spaghetti sauce

Toppings (see listing)

Shredded cheese, mozzarella or your choice

Grated Parmesan cheese

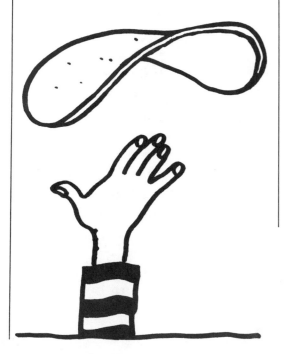

HERE'S WHAT YOU DO:

1 Preheat oven to 375°.

2 Spray pizza pan or cookie sheet with no-stick spray. Prepare crust according to package directions.

3 Spread a thin layer of sauce over crust.

4 Top with various toppings of your choice. Then sprinkle on shredded and grated cheese.

5 Bake at 375° in oven for about 10 minutes, depending on type of crust and the amount of toppings you are using.

Makes enough for 4 to 6 people.

Pizza Toppings

Here are some possible pizza toppings to get you started, but we're sure you can add lots of ideas of your own. The main thing is to be sure that the toppers match. If you use a strong flavor like sausage or pepperoni, then you probably won't want another strong flavor like blue cheese — but then, it's up to you!

Mushrooms, sliced (canned are fine)

Peppers, sliced

Black olives, sliced

Cooked bacon, crumbled

Onions, sliced

Hamburger meat, browned

Pepperoni, sliced thin

Blue cheese, crumbled

Cheddar cheese, shredded

Artichoke hearts, sliced

Sun-dried tomatoes

Fresh parsley, dill, basil

Sausage, cooked and crumbled

Chicken, cooked and sliced

FAUX LASAGNA

*Have you ever heard of faux pearls? They're fake pearls that look just like the real things. Well, **Faux Lasagna** isn't really lasagna, but it tastes just like the real thing and it is a lot easier to make.*

HERE'S WHAT YOU NEED:

1 small onion, chopped

1 green pepper, chopped

1 tablespoon margarine

1 pound hamburger meat

1 jar (8 ounces) tomato sauce or spaghetti sauce

1 package (8 ounces) wide egg noodles

1 package (8 ounces) whipped cream cheese

1 small container sour cream

1 container (8 ounces) cottage cheese, or ricotta cheese

Shredded mozzarella cheese

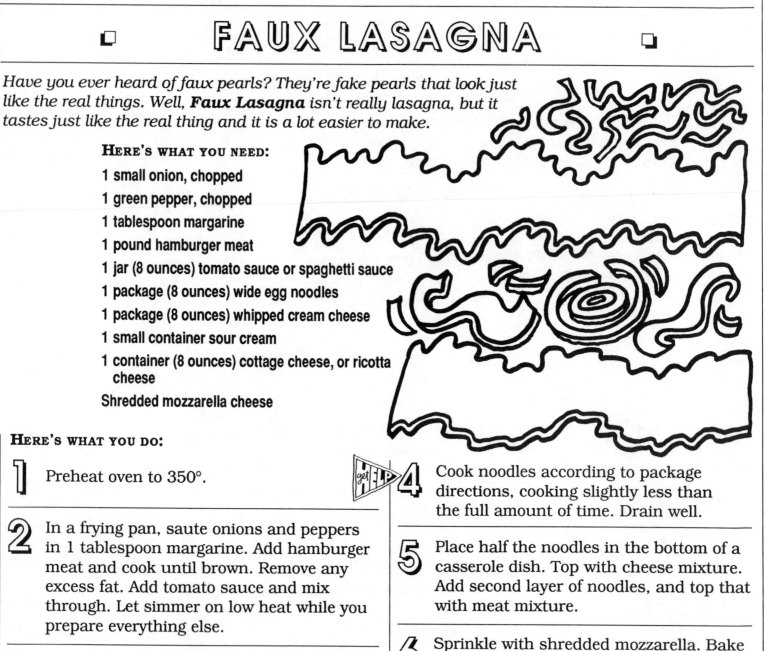

HERE'S WHAT YOU DO:

1 Preheat oven to 350°.

2 In a frying pan, saute onions and peppers in 1 tablespoon margarine. Add hamburger meat and cook until brown. Remove any excess fat. Add tomato sauce and mix through. Let simmer on low heat while you prepare everything else.

3 In a bowl, mix together the cream cheese, sour cream, and cottage cheese.

4 Cook noodles according to package directions, cooking slightly less than the full amount of time. Drain well.

5 Place half the noodles in the bottom of a casserole dish. Top with cheese mixture. Add second layer of noodles, and top that with meat mixture.

6 Sprinkle with shredded mozzarella. Bake at 350° for 30 minutes or until bubbly.

Makes enough for 6 people.

CHILI CON CARNE

Many people are famous for their chili recipes. This is one that our mom has been making for a long, long time. It isn't really spicy (but you can add more chili powder if your family likes it that way), but it is really good.

HERE'S WHAT YOU NEED:

2 medium onions, sliced

1 large green pepper, sliced

2 pounds hamburger meat

1 large can red kidney beans, drained (or 2 smaller cans)

1 can stewed tomatoes

1 can tomato sauce

1 teaspoon sugar

1 teaspoon oregano

1/4 teaspoon paprika

1 tablespoon chili powder

HERE'S WHAT YOU DO:

1 In a large frying pan, brown the onion and pepper.

2 Add the hamburger, crumble, and cook on medium heat for 5 minutes or until browned. Remove any excess fat. Put the meat in a large casserole dish that can go on top of the stove.

3 Add the drained kidney beans, stewed tomatoes, tomato sauce, sugar, oregano, paprika, and chili powder.

4 Mix well. Heat through and serve hot with *Homemade Corn Bread* (see page 80).

Makes enough for 8 people.

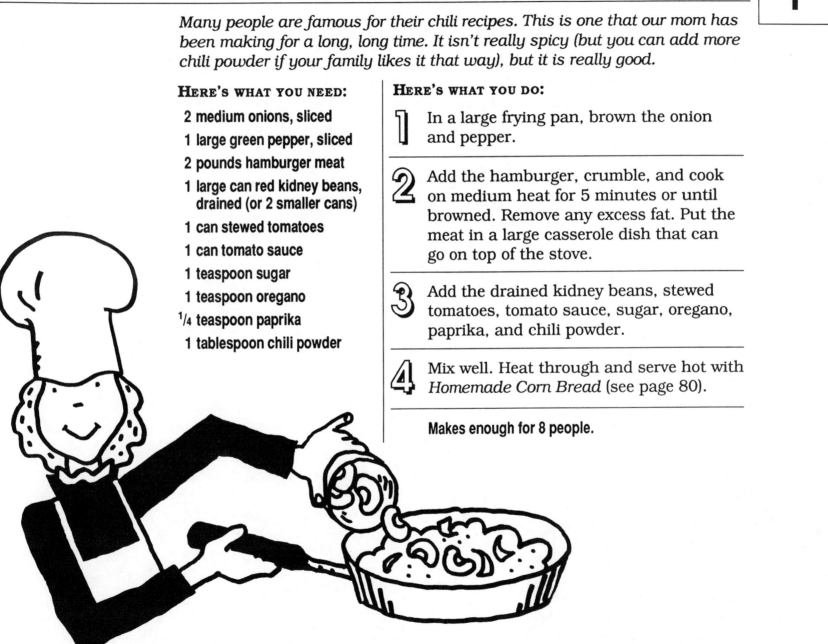

RUTH'S STEW

If you think you don't like stew, try this. It is really good on a cold night. If it's your turn to make dinner, you can begin this when you get home from school, and let it cook in the oven until everyone is home for dinner. If someone has time, **Baking Powder Biscuits** *(see page 79) or* **Homemade Corn Bread** *(see page 80) go very well with this meal.*

HERE'S WHAT YOU NEED:

2 pounds of stew beef, cut up into big chunks

1 teaspoon salt

1 tablespoon sugar

3 tablespoons Minute™ tapioca

1 can (8 ounces) of tomatoes

1/2 cup bread crumbs

3 onions, peeled and cut into quarters

3 carrots, peeled and cut into 3-inch chunks

1 cup celery, sliced thin

HERE'S WHAT YOU DO:

1 Preheat oven to 300°.

2 Combine all ingredients in a large casserole dish, including the juice from the canned tomatoes. Mix well.

3 Bake in oven at 300° for 3 hours. Stir occasionally during cooking time. If stew seems too dry, add 1/3 cup orange juice.

Makes enough for 8 people.

Note: You can add 4 scrubbed potatoes, cut into quarters, for the last hour of cooking. That way you will have a complete meal in the stew pot.

EASY GREEN BEAN CASSEROLE

If it's your turn to make dinner, here is the easiest way that we know to round out a meal, and the best thing is, it tastes delicious!

HERE'S WHAT YOU NEED:

2 packages (20 ounces each) frozen green beans

1 can (18.5 ounces) concentrated mushroom soup

1 can dried onion rings

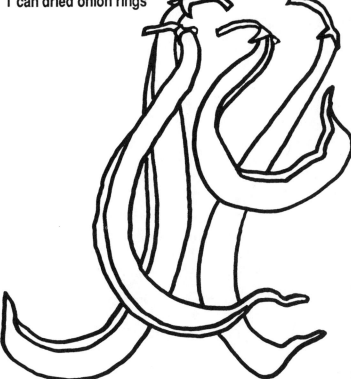

HERE'S WHAT YOU DO:

1 Preheat the oven to 350°.

2 Cook the green beans according to the directions. Don't overcook because you are going to bake them also.

3 Drain beans very well and put in a casserole dish.

4 Add the mushroom soup concentrate (don't add any water).

5 Gently mix together within the dish.

6 Sprinkle the onion rings on top.

7 Cover and bake at 350° for 30 minutes, or until beans begin to bubble.

8 Be sure to serve while still hot.

Makes enough for 6 people.

GRILLED VEGETABLES

The simplest and easiest summer dinners seem to be those that are barbecued. Sometimes just grilling chicken or fish along with this vegetable recipe makes a perfect dinner.

HERE'S WHAT YOU NEED:

1 green pepper, sliced lengthwise and seeded

1 red pepper, sliced lengthwise

1 large Spanish onion, sliced in rounds

2 small zucchini, sliced in strips

1 cup salad dressing such as Italian, vinaigrette, or your choice (not creamy style)

HERE'S WHAT YOU DO:

1 Prepare vegetables as directed.

2 Place in dish and marinate in salad dressing about ½ hour or longer.

3 If you have a special grill that doesn't allow small foods to slip into fire, use it. Otherwise, place aluminum foil with lots of holes poked in it on the grill. Place vegetables on grill after the meat is cooked.

4 Cook for 5 to 10 minutes until crisp tender and browned. Serve hot.

Makes enough for 4 people.

APRICOT KUGLE

Our Grandma Golde has been making this for years. "Kugle" is a word for a noodle casserole, and this one is delicious.

HERE'S WHAT YOU NEED:

1 box (8 ounces) egg noodles
1/2 pound cream cheese
1 stick margarine
3 eggs
1/2 cup sugar
12 ounces of apricot nectar (juice)
1 cup sour cream

Topping:
3/4 cups corn flakes
1/4 cup brown sugar
4 tablespoons margarine, melted
Dash of cinnamon

HERE'S WHAT YOU DO:

1 Preheat oven to 350°.

2 Cook egg noodles according to directions on box. Drain well.

3 Cream the margarine and cream cheese together in a large bowl.

4 Add the remaining ingredients including the noodles (not the topping). Mix well.

5 Pour into a 9" x 9" baking dish.

6 In a separate bowl, combine all of the topping ingredients.

7 Sprinkle the topping over the noodle mixture.

8 Bake at 350° for 45 minutes.

Makes enough for 8 people.

RICE CASSEROLE

The combination of the rice and the onion soup makes a very flavorful, very easy-to-make casserole.

HERE'S WHAT YOU NEED:

1 package dry onion soup mix

1 tablespoon margarine

1 cup regular brown or white rice (not instant)

2 cups water

HERE'S WHAT YOU DO:

1 Preheat oven to 375°.

2 Bring water and margarine to a boil. Add soup mix and rice.

3 Pour into a small casserole dish.

4 Bake covered at 375° for 45 minutes.

Makes enough for about 8 people.

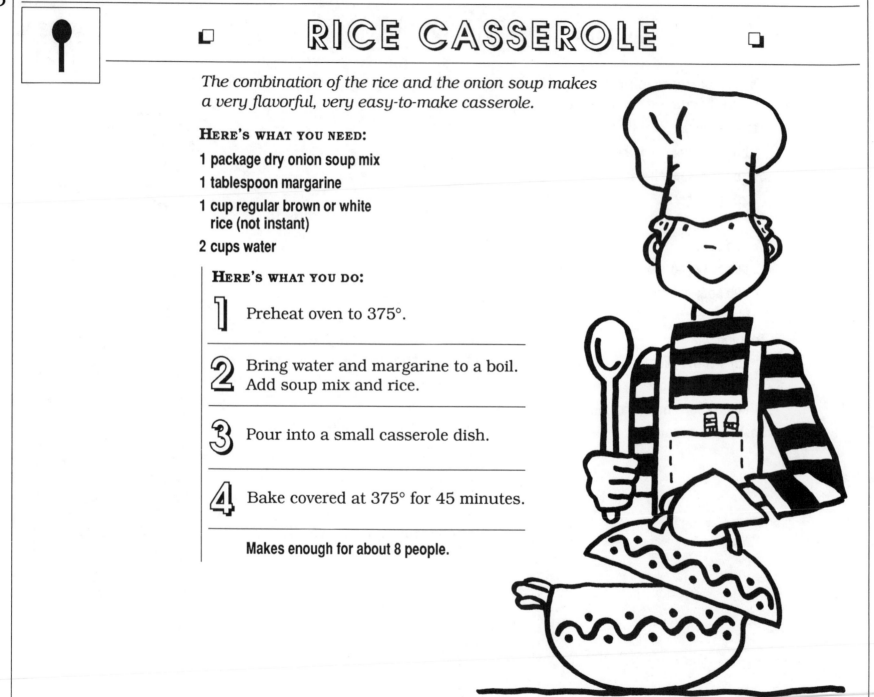

AUNT LINDA'S FAMOUS MACARONI & CHEESE

This dish has always been a great treat, and Zach especially enjoys it when our Aunt Linda prepares it.

HERE'S WHAT YOU NEED:

1 pound elbow macaroni

2 tablespoons margarine

1³/₄ cups milk

4 to 6 ounces extra sharp cheddar, sliced

4 to 6 ounces Velveeta®, sliced

HERE'S WHAT YOU DO:

1 Preheat oven to 350°.

 get HELP

2 Cook the macaroni according to the package directions. Drain and pour into a large casserole dish.

3 In a large saucepan, melt the margarine. Add the milk and heat through.

4 Add both cheeses. Mix over medium heat, until all of the cheese is melted.

5 Pour the warm cheese mixture over the cooked macaroni.

6 Mix until all the noodles are coated with the sauce.

7 Bake at 350° until hot, about 10 to 15 minutes.

Makes enough for 8 people.

CREAMY ASPARAGUS & CARROTS

This is a great way to prepare vegetables. It's easy enough so that you can make this at the last minute. Try the basic recipe with another combination of vegetables, too.

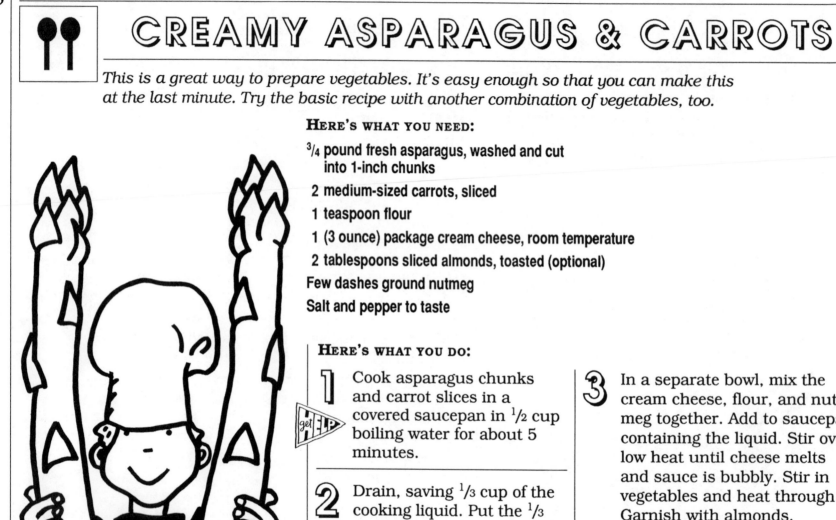

HERE'S WHAT YOU NEED:

3/4 **pound fresh asparagus, washed and cut into 1-inch chunks**

2 **medium-sized carrots, sliced**

1 **teaspoon flour**

1 **(3 ounce) package cream cheese, room temperature**

2 **tablespoons sliced almonds, toasted (optional)**

Few dashes ground nutmeg

Salt and pepper to taste

HERE'S WHAT YOU DO:

1 Cook asparagus chunks and carrot slices in a covered saucepan in ¹/₂ cup boiling water for about 5 minutes.

get HELP

2 Drain, saving ¹/₃ cup of the cooking liquid. Put the ¹/₃ cup liquid back into the saucepan.

3 In a separate bowl, mix the cream cheese, flour, and nutmeg together. Add to saucepan containing the liquid. Stir over low heat until cheese melts and sauce is bubbly. Stir in vegetables and heat through. Garnish with almonds.

Makes enough for 6 people.

MARMALADE CHICKEN

*This has been a family favorite for years. For the easiest special birthday dinner ever, prepare this chicken with **Creamy Asparagus and Carrots** (see page 118) and **Baked Potatoes** (see page 82).*

HERE'S WHAT YOU NEED:

1 bottle (8 ounces) of Russian salad dressing (Use Wishbone™ — not the creamy kind)

1 package dry onion soup mix

1 jar (10 ounces) marmalade or apricot preserves

1 package of chicken pieces, a cut-up fryer is good, about 3 pounds

HERE'S WHAT YOU DO:

1 Preheat oven to 350°.

2 Wash the chicken and pat dry. Place in a baking pan in a single layer.

3 Combine all remaining ingredients in a bowl and mix well. Pour the sauce over the chicken. (If you are cooking a smaller amount of chicken, you can save the extra sauce in the refrigerator for a few weeks.)

4 Bake chicken covered with aluminum foil at 350° for 50 minutes.

5 Uncover the chicken, spoon the sauce over the top of the chicken, and continue to bake for another 30 minutes.

Makes enough for 6 people.

NUTRI·NOTE

Children need extra calories for energy. Instead of counting calories to lose weight, just get out there and exercise or participate in some sports. It's a lot easier, healthier, and more fun, too.

CHICKEN & BROCCOLI CASSEROLE

Our Great Aunt Lois is a very good cook, and we have always liked visiting her home. Here's one of her recipes that we hope you enjoy.

HERE'S WHAT YOU NEED:

3 boneless chicken breasts, cut in half lengthwise

2 packages (10 ounces each) broccoli spears, or equal amount of fresh broccoli

Sauce:

2 cans cream of chicken soup, no water added

1 cup plain yogurt (or sour cream)

1 teaspoon lemon juice

1/2 teaspoon curry powder

1/3 cup orange juice

Topping:

1/2 cup bread crumbs

1 tablespoon margarine, melted

1/2 cup shredded cheddar

HERE'S WHAT YOU DO:

1 Preheat oven to 350°. Place chicken in a 7" x 11" baking dish and bake for 20 minutes.

2 While chicken is baking, cook broccoli according to package directions, but for only 3 to 4 minutes (not the full time). Drain.

3 Prepare sauce by mixing all of the ingredients together in a bowl.

4 To prepare bread crumbs for topping, melt margarine and mix with the bread crumbs in a separate small bowl.

5 Remove chicken from oven and place it on a plate. Place partially cooked broccoli on the bottom of the baking dish (don't burn yourself). Then place the chicken on top of the broccoli. Next, pour the sauce over the whole thing.

6 Top first with shredded cheese and sprinkle the bread crumbs over all. Bake uncovered at 350° for 30 minutes. Serve hot with rice.

Makes enough for 5 to 6 people.

CHICKEN STIR-FRY

This is one of Sarah's specialties. For a stir-fry, food is cooked quickly in very little oil. The idea is for the vegetables to be very crisp, so add the vegetables that need the least cooking toward the very end. For a vegetarian stir-fry, leave out the chicken and add some of the other vegetables suggested below.

HERE'S WHAT YOU NEED:

1 whole boneless breast of chicken, pounded and then sliced

1 clove garlic, minced

3 teaspoons vegetable oil

$\frac{1}{2}$ green pepper, thinly sliced

$\frac{1}{2}$ red pepper, thinly sliced

1 small onion, diced

2 mushrooms, sliced

$\frac{1}{2}$ cup fresh snow peas (if you use frozen, thaw and then add them at the very last minute)

3 teaspoons soy sauce

HERE'S WHAT YOU DO:

1 Prepare all of the ingredients according to directions above.

2 In a large frying pan on medium-high heat, brown the garlic in the oil.

3 Add the chicken pieces and cook quickly, turning to brown both sides.

4 When chicken is cooked, remove it from pan and add the peppers and onions. When crisp tender, add the mushrooms and snow peas and stir-fry 1 minute more. Vegetables should still be colorful.

5 Return chicken to the pan. Add soy sauce and toss with vegetables.

Makes enough for 2 to 3 people.

Note: Stir-frying is very versatile. You can add any vegetables you want, or substitute thinly sliced steak, pork, or shrimp for the chicken. You can add broccoli, celery, carrots, cherry tomatoes, canned water chestnuts, or bamboo shoots. It is usually served with rice, but it is also good when served with egg noodles.

CHICKEN CORDON BLEU

We're sure there are very fancy recipes for this famous chicken dish, but we think it tastes fine cooked this easy way.

HERE'S WHAT YOU NEED:

Boneless chicken breasts, one half breast per serving

Margarine

Swiss cheese slices, or cheese of your choice

Ham slices

1 can cream of chicken or cream of mushroom soup, condensed

½ pint sour cream

HERE'S WHAT YOU DO:

1 Preheat oven to 350°. Butter the bottom of a baking dish.

2 Wash the chicken and pat dry. If using whole breasts, cut the pieces in half lengthwise.

3 In a medium-sized frying pan, brown chicken in some margarine over medium heat until golden brown on both sides.

4 Place the browned chicken in the casserole dish. Cover generously with a layer of ham slices and then a layer of cheese slices.

5 Pour the soup (don't add water) and sour cream into the frying pan, and mix it well. Then pour the mixture over the cheese.

6 Bake uncovered at 350° for about 40 minutes.

Makes as many servings as you like, one-half chicken breast per serving.

Note: You can prepare this right before you bake it, or you can refrigerate it uncooked for as long as 24 hours before you bake it. This is also good without the soup and sour cream sauce. Simply bake until chicken is cooked and cheese is melted.

do you know?

Proteins are made up of 20 different building blocks called *amino acids*. Kids and adults alike need to have the right balance of amino acids in order for the protein they eat to be "complete" and therefore usable by their bodies.

Animal foods, such as meat, eggs, cheese, and milk, contain all of the right amounts of amino acids and are therefore, *complete proteins*. However, it is possible to get complete protein through vegetable combinations, rather than just through animal foods.

OVEN-FRIED CHICKEN

We like fried chicken but we aren't allowed to deep-fry anything in hot oil. This is almost as good as fried chicken plus it's safer to prepare and a lot healthier to eat.

HERE'S WHAT YOU NEED:

1 cup flour

2 teaspoons salt

$1/4$ teaspoon pepper

2 teaspoons paprika

$1/2$ cup vegetable oil

1 cut-up frying chicken

SAFETY ALERT!

Smother a pan fire with a lid. Never use water.

HERE'S WHAT YOU DO:

1 Preheat oven to 425°.

2 Mix flour, salt, pepper, and paprika in a paper bag.

3 Shake 3 or 4 pieces of chicken at a time in the bag. This will allow every piece to be coated thoroughly.

4 Pour the vegetable oil in a 13" x 9 $1/2$" pan, and place coated chicken in the oil.

5 Bake about 30 minutes.

6 Turn over and bake another 30 minutes or until chicken is crisp and tender.

Makes enough for 4 to 6 people.

QUICK & EASY FISH FILLETS

If you are a fish fan, try this recipe. It is good and simple to prepare.

HERE'S WHAT YOU NEED:

2 to 3 pounds fish fillets, sole, halibut, or your choice

Margarine or oil

1 cup flour

2 cups bread crumbs

1 teaspoon nutmeg

2 eggs

2 tablespoons lemon juice

HERE'S WHAT YOU DO:

1. Combine the flour, bread crumbs, and nutmeg in a shallow bowl.

2. Mix the eggs and lemon juice together. Then, dip the fish fillets first into the egg mixture and then into the flour mixture, covering well.

3. Heat the margarine in a skillet and quickly fry the fillets for about 3 minutes on each side, adding more margarine if you need.

Makes enough for 6 servings.

PORK CHOPS WITH APPLES

Here's a very easy way to prepare pork chops. If it is your turn to prepare dinner, you can make this after school, put it in the oven, and it will be ready at dinnertime.

HERE'S WHAT YOU NEED:

6 pork chops

2 tablespoons vegetable oil or margarine

3 to 4 unpeeled apples, cored and sliced

$\frac{1}{2}$ cup brown sugar, packed down

$\frac{1}{2}$ teaspoon cinnamon

2 tablespoons margarine

HERE'S WHAT YOU DO:

1. Preheat oven to 400°.

2. In a skillet, brown the pork chops on both sides in the oil or margarine.

3. Place the apple slices in a greased baking dish. Sprinkle on the brown sugar and the cinnamon. Dot with bits of margarine. Layer pork chops on top of all.

4. Bake at 400°, covered (you can use aluminum foil if dish doesn't have a cover), for $1\frac{1}{2}$ hours.

Makes enough for 6 people.

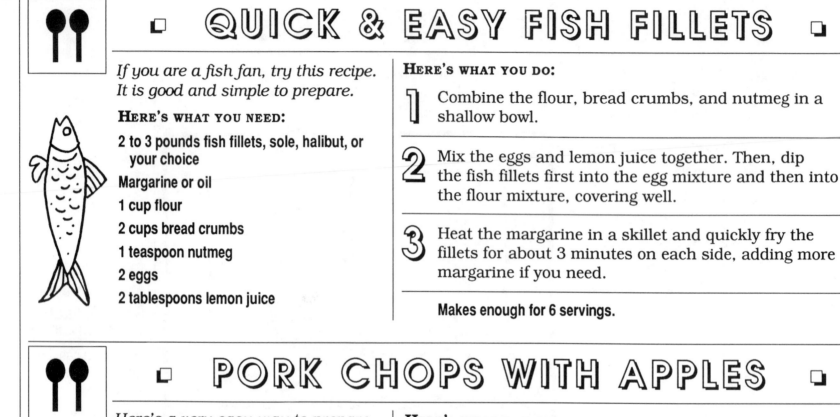

FETTUCCINE PARMESAN

This recipe is a little more difficult than some of the others in this book, but once you try it, you'll want to make it often because it is very good. There is a quicker, easier version of this recipe on the next page.

HERE'S WHAT YOU NEED:

About ¹/₂ pound fresh spinach fettuccine or other pasta

2 tablespoons margarine

3 tablespoons flour

2 cups milk

¹/₂ **cup heavy cream**

¹/₂ **cup Parmesan cheese**

Pepper

HERE'S WHAT YOU DO:

1 Set a large pot of water on the stove to come to a boil while you prepare the sauce.

2 In a medium-sized saucepan, melt the margarine and stir in the flour.

3 Cook for 1 minute over medium heat, while mixture begins to bubble slightly.

4 Very slowly, add the milk and heavy cream, stirring constantly with a wire whisk. Continue stirring until mixture begins to bubble and thicken.

5 Stir in the Parmesan cheese and continue to stir until it melts. Season with pepper. Lower heat to low setting.

6 Cook the pasta according to package directions. Drain well.

7 Pour the sauce over the pasta and toss.

8 The sauce and the pasta both must be hot for this to taste good, so call people to the table right before the pasta is done cooking.

Makes enough for 5 to 6 people.

SAFETY ALERT!

Cooking pasta:
Cooking pasta is easy, but it is also dangerous. Pasta has to cook in a lot of boiling water. Be sure to have an adult with you because lots of times the boiling water "boils over" while the pasta is cooking. Also, please have an adult carry the pasta over to the sink to drain in a colander. Once the steam clears, you can do the rest yourself.

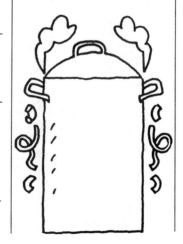

EASY PASTA WITH A CREAMY CHEESE SAUCE

*This isn't as creamy as the **Fettuccine Parmesan** recipe, but it is very good and very easy to prepare. You can use any kind of pasta, so why not try some angel hair pasta or small shells.*

HERE'S WHAT YOU NEED:

About 1 pound pasta, your choice

1 stick (8 tablespoons) margarine

$\frac{1}{4}$ cup heavy cream

1 cup Parmesan cheese, grated

Pepper

HERE'S WHAT YOU DO:

1 Cook the pasta according to the package directions. Drain well.

2 Pour the pasta into a large bowl and quickly add the margarine, heavy cream, and about half of the Parmesan cheese.

3 Toss until well mixed.

4 Serve immediately topped with pepper and the remaining cheese.

Makes enough for 5 to 6 people.

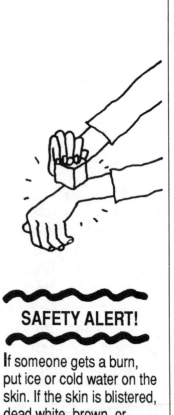

SAFETY ALERT!

If someone gets a burn, put ice or cold water on the skin. If the skin is blistered, dead white, brown, or charred, the burn is very serious and you must call for emergency help.

DYNAMITE DESSERTS

Without even counting, it is our guess that we have more dessert recipes than any other type in this book. It seems that most everyone loves desserts, and very often, when we have friends over and can't think of what to do, we end up baking some cookies or a cake. So yes, we have had many opportunities to perfect these recipes over the years!

We learned a lot about baking from our Grandma Golde. She started baking with us when we were just little kids, and she always taught us some "tricks of the trade." We've tried to pass a lot of them on to you here.

If you baby-sit, baking can be a nice way to spend some time with younger children. They love to mix and stir, pat, press, decorate, and most of all, eat these wonderful treats. Save plenty for the adults when they get home . . . . after all, we know that grown-ups like desserts just as much as anyone!

STRAWBERRY SHORTCAKE

We have had this dessert for years on Father's Day. In fact, **Strawberry Shortcake** *is a favorite all through strawberry season.*

HERE'S WHAT YOU NEED:

$2^{1}/_{3}$ cups Bisquick® baking mix

$^{1}/_{2}$ cup milk

3 tablespoons sugar

3 tablespoons margarine, melted

1 quart (or more) of sliced strawberries

Homemade Whipped Cream (see page 97)

HERE'S WHAT YOU DO:

1. Preheat oven to 425°.

2. In a large bowl, mix all of the ingredients, except the strawberries and whipped cream, until a soft dough forms.

3. Place the dough in a square 9" x 9" pan, ungreased.

4. Bake until surface is golden brown, about 15 minutes.

5. Cool in the pan for 10 minutes before serving.

6. Top each serving with lots of sliced strawberries and *Homemade Whipped Cream.*

Makes enough for 6 to 8 people.

FRUITFUL PIZZA

Every summer our neighbors gather together for a big picnic. The year that Mrs. Clark brought this dessert, we knew we wanted the recipe.

HERE'S WHAT YOU NEED:

- 1 box sugar cookie mix or a package of Pillsbury™ sugar cookie dough, or homemade sugar cookie dough
- 1 package (8 ounces) cream cheese
- 1/4 cup sugar
- Blueberries, washed and hulled
- Strawberries, washed, hulled, and halved
- Kiwi fruit, peeled and sliced
- Green grapes, washed

Glaze:

- 1 cup orange juice
- 2 tablespoons sugar
- 2 tablespoons cornstarch

HERE'S WHAT YOU DO:

1 Preheat oven to 350°.

2 To make dough, follow the directions on the box of the cookie mix or open roll of cookie dough. Spread dough in a greased pizza pan and bake at 350° for 15 minutes, or until light brown. Remove from oven and cool on pan. (If you don't have a pizza pan, use a cookie sheet.)

3 In a bowl, mix the cream cheese and the sugar with a mixer. Spread over the cooled cookie-pizza crust.

4 Arrange all of the fruit slices and pieces on top of the cream cheese mixture. Try making a pattern or a design of some sort.

5 In a saucepan, combine the glaze ingredients and bring to a boil until thickened.

6 Carefully spread the glaze over the entire fruit pizza. Keep refrigerated until you are ready to serve. Slice like a pizza.

Makes 8 to 12 slices.

FOURTH OF JULY CAKE

CLASSY COOKS

Separating Eggs. To separate the egg white from the egg yolk, crack the egg hard against the side of a small bowl. Carefully open the egg so that the whole yolk is in one half of the shell. Spill out the white that is in the other half of the shell. Then gently pour the yolk into the empty shell half, letting the white slip out into the bowl. Do this a few times and you will have only the yolk left in the shell, and the white in the bowl. It is really quite easy to do. Remember: Always put the whites in a separate bowl and work over a small separate dish. That way if you goof up on one egg, you won't have spoiled the ones you did right.

Mrs. Raabe, a friend of the family, bakes a beautiful, fancy **Fourth of July Cake** *every year when our families have a picnic together. This is our easier variation of her good idea — a cake that looks like the American flag. It's a lot of fun to decorate, and a lot of fun to eat.*

HERE'S WHAT YOU NEED:

2¼ cups cake flour

1½ cups sugar

  3 teaspoons baking powder

  1 teaspoon salt

½ cup soft shortening
  (margarine or Crisco™)

  1 cup milk

1½ teaspoons vanilla extract

  2 eggs

Topping:

  2 cups strawberries, washed, dried, and halved

½ cup blueberries, washed and dried

HERE'S WHAT YOU DO:

1 Preheat oven to 350°.

2 Blend flour, sugar, baking powder, and salt together.

3 Add shortening, ⅔ cup of the milk, and the vanilla extract. Blend thoroughly.

4 Add the rest of the milk (⅓ cup) and the eggs. Blend thoroughly.

5 Pour into a greased 10" by 15" pan. Bake for 35 minutes at 350°.

6 While the cake is in the oven, prepare the frosting (see Cream Cheese Frosting, page 150).

7 When the cake is golden brown, remove from the oven. Cool for at least 45 minutes before frosting. Be careful not to break open the surface of the cake while spreading on the icing. If the icing is too thick, add a little cream, one teaspoon at a time.

8 Wait to decorate the cake until just before serving. Be sure the fruit is very dry or it will run onto the icing. Using the white background, arrange the strawberries into the red stripes of the American flag, and the blueberries as the field of blue.

Makes 1 sheet cake.

AUTUMN APPLE CRISP

There are so many ways to make this that you can actually create your own recipe. Some people like to use granola, raisins, or rolled oats in their crisps. Whatever recipe you create, always be sure to top it with vanilla ice cream or whipped cream.

HERE'S WHAT YOU NEED:

6 large apples, peeled, cored, and sliced

$\frac{1}{4}$ teaspoon cinnamon

$\frac{1}{4}$ cup water

1 teaspoon lemon juice

Topping:

1 cup brown sugar

$\frac{3}{4}$ cup flour

1 cup margarine

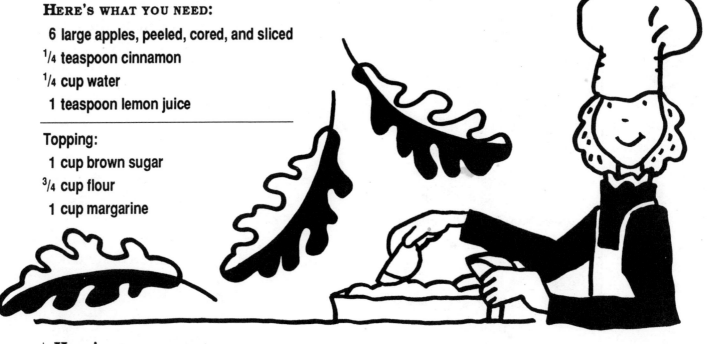

HERE'S WHAT YOU DO:

1 Preheat oven to 350°.

2 Grease an 8" or 9" square pan. Place apples in it and add $\frac{1}{4}$ cup water. Then sprinkle on cinnamon and lemon juice.

3 Prepare topping by crumbling the margarine, flour, and brown sugar together with your hands in a bowl. Work fast so the margarine doesn't melt from your warm hands. You want a crumbly mixture.

4 Sprinkle the crumbs over the apples. Bake at 350° for about 30 minutes or until apples are bubbling in the pan. Serve warm.

Makes enough for 8 people.

◻ SARAH'S LEMON POUND CAKE ◻

Our Grandma Eleanor says this is a real treat. It has a nice lemon flavor, and the glaze gives it a nice touch of sweetness.

HERE'S WHAT YOU NEED:

$2\frac{1}{4}$ cups flour

3 eggs

2 sticks margarine

2 cups sugar

$\frac{1}{4}$ teaspoon salt

$\frac{1}{2}$ teaspoon baking soda

$\frac{1}{8}$ teaspoon lemon juice

1 teaspoon vanilla extract

1 teaspoon grated lemon peel

1 cup sour cream

Glaze:

$1\frac{1}{4}$ cups confectioners' sugar

$\frac{1}{4}$ cup lemon juice

1 teaspoon vanilla extract

HERE'S WHAT YOU DO:

1 Preheat oven to 325°.

2 Combine all of the ingredients for the cake (not the glaze) in a large bowl and mix very well with a mixer.

3 Pour into a well-greased bundt cake pan. Bake at 325° for 1 hour.

4 Mix the glaze ingredients together in a small bowl.

5 While the cake is still slightly warm, remove the cake from the pan. Spread the glaze on the top and let it drip down the sides of the cake. Add a little water (one teaspoon at a time) if the glaze gets too thick to drip.

Makes 1 cake.

CLASSY COOKS

What's a bundt pan? It is a special cake pan that makes a tall cake. The pan often has a design in the sides and it has a hollow tube down the middle. If you don't have one, you can bake these cakes in a sponge cake pan, but check them early as they might not take as long to bake. Inexpensive bundt cake pans are usually sold in supermarkets, so maybe you can tempt someone to help you pay for one by promising to bake *Sarah's Lemon Pound Cake* or the *Chocolate Chip Bundt Cake.*

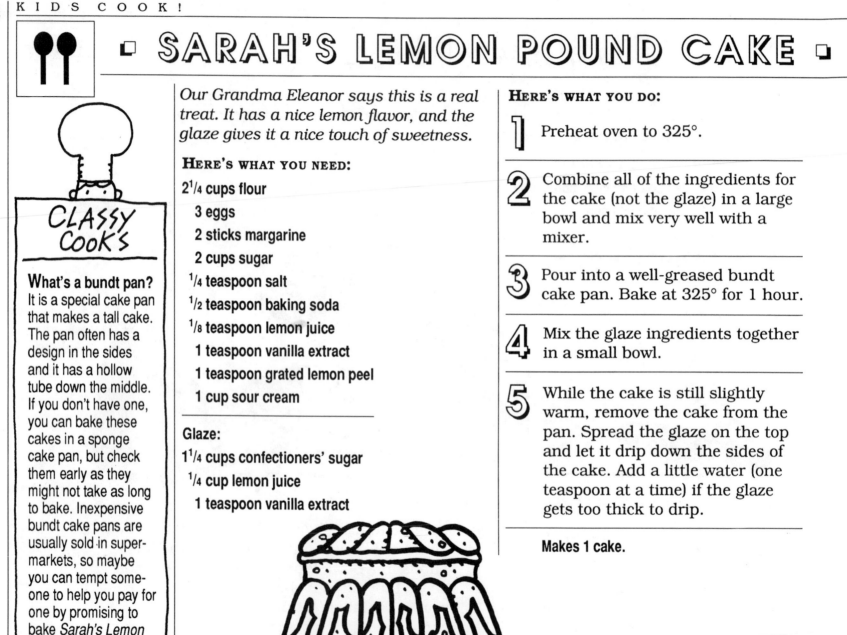

BROWNIE PIE

This easy-to-make chocolate pie tastes just like a chewy, homemade brownie. The best way to enjoy this is topped with a big scoop of your favorite ice cream. If you want to make a really super dessert, add some **Easy Hot Fudge Sauce** and some **Homemade Whipped Cream.**

HERE'S WHAT YOU NEED:

1 cup sugar

$1/2$ cup margarine

2 eggs, separated (see "How to separate eggs," page 130)

2 ounces unsweetened chocolate, melted, then slightly cooled

$1/3$ cup flour

1 teaspoon vanilla extract

$1/8$ teaspoon salt

HERE'S WHAT YOU DO:

1 Preheat oven to 325°.

2 In a bowl, cream together the sugar and margarine.

3 Separate the two eggs, saving both the whites and yolks in separate small bowls. (See "How to separate eggs," page 130.) Beat the egg yolks and the melted chocolate into the creamed margarine mixture.

4 Add the flour and mix well.

5 In a separate bowl, whip together the egg whites and the salt, until the whites form stiff peaks. Then, gently fold in the egg whites to the flour mix.

6 Pour into a greased 8" pie pan, and bake at 325° for about 30 minutes.

7 Cool and serve with ice cream.

Makes enough for 6 to 8 people.

SAFETY ALERT!

Don't overload electrical outlets or leave cords where children can pull on them.

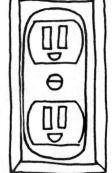

CHOCOLATE SURPRISE CUPCAKES

These cupcakes are so good and so special that no one will believe that you made them yourself. They are better than anything you can buy in a bakery.

HERE'S WHAT YOU NEED:

3 cups flour

2 cups sugar

1/2 cup unsweetened cocoa powder

2 teaspoons baking soda

2 cups water

2/3 cup vegetable oil

2 tablespoons cider vinegar

2 teaspoons vanilla extract

Filling:

1 package (8 ounces) cream cheese

1 egg

1/3 cup sugar

Pinch of salt

1 package (6 ounces) chocolate chips

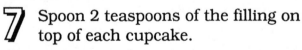

HERE'S WHAT YOU DO:

1 Preheat the oven to 350°.

2 Lightly grease muffin pans or put in paper cupcake liners (makes 18, so make two batches).

3 In a large bowl, sift together the flour, sugar, cocoa, and the baking soda.

4 Add to the mixture, the water, oil, vanilla, and vinegar. Beat at medium speed for about 3 minutes. Set aside.

5 To make the filling, in another bowl, cream the cream cheese with a spoon. Add the egg, sugar, and the salt. Beat until smooth. Fold in the chocolate chips.

6 Fill each muffin cup about 2/3 full with the chocolate batter.

7 Spoon 2 teaspoons of the filling on top of each cupcake.

8 Bake at 350° for about 20 minutes or until the cakes spring back when lightly touched.

9 Cool and serve at room temperature.

Makes about 18 cupcakes.

HIDDEN SECRET APPLE CAKE

When the leaves are turning bright colors as they do where we live in Vermont, apples are a big part of the menu. Here's a very easy and delicious apple cake that is great served with ice cream.

HERE'S WHAT YOU NEED:

8 medium-sized apples, any kind, peeled and sliced

Sugar

Cinnamon

¾ cup margarine, melted

1 cup sugar

1 cup flour

1 egg

Pinch of salt

½ cup chopped nuts (optional)

HERE'S WHAT YOU DO:

1 Preheat oven to 350°.

2 Fill a 9" or 10" pie dish about ⅔ full with sliced apples. Sprinkle sugar and cinnamon over the top of the apples (to taste and depending on how sweet or tart your apples are).

3 In a bowl, combine melted margarine, 1 cup sugar, flour, egg, salt, and chopped nuts. Mix very well, and pour over the apples.

4 Bake at 350° for about 45 minutes or until golden brown. Serve warm with ice cream.

Makes 6 to 8 slices.

CHOCOLATE CHIP BUNDT CAKE

Grandma Golde serves this whenever a guest steps through the door.
It is very easy to make and always tastes great.

HERE'S WHAT YOU NEED:

- **1 package yellow cake mix**
- **1 package (3.9 ounces) instant chocolate pudding**
- **1 cup sour cream**
- **4 eggs**
- **$\frac{1}{2}$ cup oil**
- **1 cup chocolate chips**
- **$\frac{1}{2}$ cup chopped nuts (optional)**
- **Confectioners' sugar**

SAFETY ALERT!

When cooking, keep small children in a playpen away from the cooking area.

HERE'S WHAT YOU DO:

1 Preheat oven to 350°.

2 With a mixer, beat together all of the ingredients, except the chocolate chips and the nuts, for about 7 minutes.

3 Add the nuts and the chocolate chips to the mixture. Beat again.

3 Pour into a well-greased bundt cake pan. Bake at 350° for 1 hour.

4 Cool and remove from pan. Sprinkle with a dusting of confectioners' sugar. (This looks best if you sift it on or put it through a strainer directly onto the cake.)

Makes 1 cake.

NO-BAKE CHOCOLATE GRAHAM CRACKER CAKE

This cake was our mother's favorite when she was a little girl. It is so easy to make that you'll want to make it often.

HERE'S WHAT YOU NEED:

28 graham crackers

1/2 cup chocolate syrup

Homemade Whipped Cream, (see page 97)

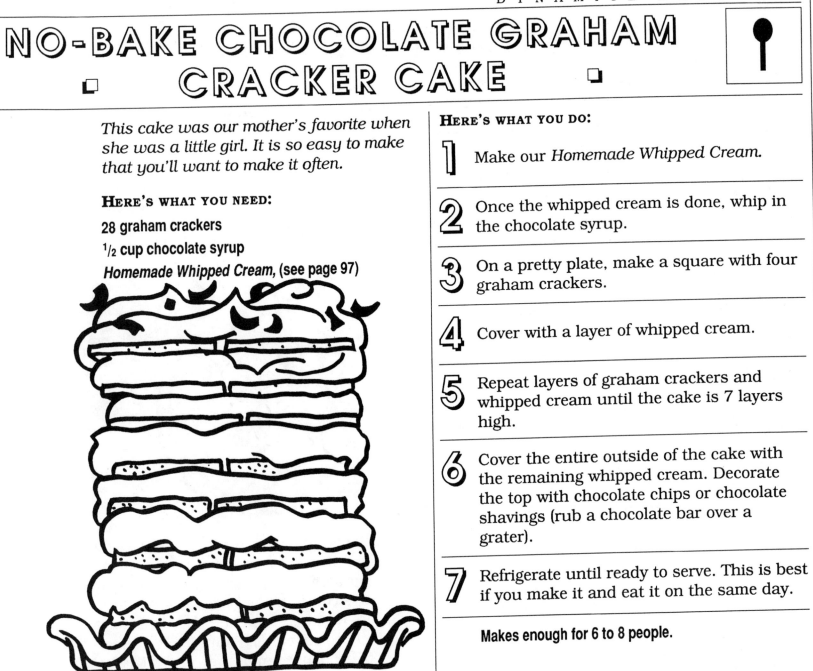

HERE'S WHAT YOU DO:

1 Make our *Homemade Whipped Cream.*

2 Once the whipped cream is done, whip in the chocolate syrup.

3 On a pretty plate, make a square with four graham crackers.

4 Cover with a layer of whipped cream.

5 Repeat layers of graham crackers and whipped cream until the cake is 7 layers high.

6 Cover the entire outside of the cake with the remaining whipped cream. Decorate the top with chocolate chips or chocolate shavings (rub a chocolate bar over a grater).

7 Refrigerate until ready to serve. This is best if you make it and eat it on the same day.

Makes enough for 6 to 8 people.

SPECIAL COMBINATION COOKIES

These layered cookies are so easy to make that they are perfect to bake with children when you are baby-sitting.

HERE'S WHAT YOU NEED:

¹/₂ cup (1 stick) margarine

1 cup graham cracker crumbs

1 cup flaked coconut

1 package (12 ounces) chocolate chips

1 can condensed milk

¹/₂ cup chopped peanuts, pecans, or walnuts

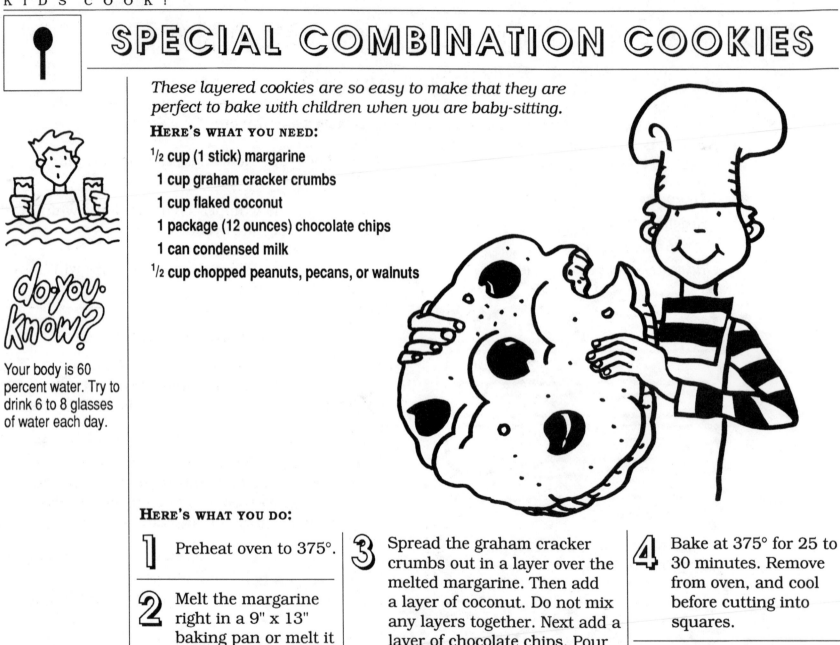

do you know?

Your body is 60 percent water. Try to drink 6 to 8 glasses of water each day.

HERE'S WHAT YOU DO:

1 Preheat oven to 375°.

2 Melt the margarine right in a 9" x 13" baking pan or melt it in a saucepan and pour into baking pan.

3 Spread the graham cracker crumbs out in a layer over the melted margarine. Then add a layer of coconut. Do not mix any layers together. Next add a layer of chocolate chips. Pour a layer of condensed milk over this, and then sprinkle a layer of nuts over all. Do not mix.

4 Bake at 375° for 25 to 30 minutes. Remove from oven, and cool before cutting into squares.

Makes about 36 squares.

CHOCOLATE CHIP CRISPERS

Grandma Golde's Baking Tips

We think our Grandma Golde's cookbook, *Golde's Homemade Cookies* has the greatest cookie recipes! She has taught us most of what we know about cooking and baking, and here are some of her baking tips which we want to share with you.

• Always measure the ingredients accurately. Baking is different than making salads and soups where you can substitute and create your own recipes. When you bake, follow the recipe carefully.

• Measure things out over the counter or a separate bowl — not the bowl you are mixing ingredients in. That way, if you spill, you won't ruin the whole recipe.

• Set out the ingredients you are going to use, and then put them away as you use them. This way you won't leave anything out, and you won't put anything in twice. (We think this is the most important tip!)

• Check to see if your cookies and cakes are done about 5 minutes early, because some ovens are "hotter" than others.

• Always remove your cookies from the cookie sheet and cool them on a wire rack. Otherwise, they continue baking on the hot pan even though they are out of the oven.

• If you have two cookie sheets, use one in the oven and one for cooling. Don't put two cookie sheets in the oven at one time.

• Cool your cakes before frosting. Otherwise, the icing melts right into the cake.

No one can improve on Original Toll House Cookies® (recipe is on back of Nestle's semisweet chocolate pieces), but we think this is another great way to bake chocolate chip cookies with a little something extra.

HERE'S WHAT YOU NEED:

- 1/2 cup margarine, softened
- 1 cup sugar
- 1 egg
- 1 teaspoon vanilla extract
- 1 1/4 cups all-purpose flour
- 1/2 teaspoon baking soda
- 1/2 teaspoon salt
- 2 cups Rice Crispies®
- 1 cup chocolate chips

HERE'S WHAT YOU DO:

1 Preheat oven to 350°.

2 In a large bowl, beat margarine and sugar until smooth. Beat in the egg and vanilla extract. Set aside.

3 In a medium bowl, combine the flour, baking soda, and salt. Mix together.

4 Add the flour mixture to the margarine mixture and mix well with a mixer. Stir in the Rice Crispies® and chocolate chips.

5 Grease a cookie sheet and drop the dough by teaspoonfuls onto the sheet about 3 inches apart. Bake at 350° for about 12 minutes or until light brown. Transfer to wire rack to cool.

Makes 2 dozen cookies

SHORT-CUT PEANUT BUTTER COOKIES

*On a cold winter's day, we rush to Sara Raabe's house to have hot **Short-Cut Peanut Butter Cookies**.*

HERE'S WHAT YOU NEED:

1 package yellow cake mix

1 cup chunky peanut butter

2 eggs

1/3 cup water

1 tablespoon flour

HERE'S WHAT YOU DO:

1 Preheat oven to 375°.

2 Combine half of the package of yellow cake mix and the peanut butter in a large bowl. Add 1/3 cup of water and the eggs.

3 Mix everything very thoroughly with a mixer.

4 Add the other half of the cake mix and mix again. The batter gets very stiff.

5 On an ungreased cookie sheet, drop batter by the teaspoonful. Leave about 3 inches between each cookie.

6 Dip a fork in some flour and make crisscross imprints in each cookie.

7 Bake the cookies at 375° for 8 to 10 minutes. Sprinkle some granulated sugar on the cookies while they are still hot. Remove them from the pan and place onto wire racks to cool.

Makes about 4 dozen cookies.

CHEESECAKE COOKIE SQUARES

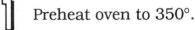

These cookies are very rich tasting, but things can get a little sticky in the preparations.

HERE'S WHAT YOU NEED:

- 2 rolls of Pillsbury® refrigerated chocolate chip cookie dough
- 1 pound cream cheese
- 2 eggs
- 1/2 cup sugar
- 1 1/2 teaspoons vanilla extract

HERE'S WHAT YOU DO:

1. Preheat oven to 350°.

2. Cut one roll of the cookie dough into 1/4"-thick slices. (Keep the other roll of dough refrigerated.)

3. Place the slices in an ungreased 9" x 13" pan, about 3 slices in each row, spacing them enough to cover the entire pan.

4. Cut a piece of waxed paper long enough to cover the entire pan and cover cookie slices. Press down on the waxed paper so that all the slices spread enough to meet each other, and cover the entire bottom of the pan. Remove the waxed paper.

5. In a bowl, blend together the cream cheese, eggs, sugar, and vanilla, until smooth.

6. Spread the cream cheese mixture evenly over the pressed cookie dough.

7. Take the remaining roll of cookie dough out of the refrigerator and slice into 1/4"-thick slices. Place slices on top of the cream cheese mixture, spacing them as close together as possible while still covering the whole top (there will be spaces).

8. Bake at 350° for 35 to 40 minutes. The top cookie dough may turn brown before it is done, so cover with tin foil.

Makes about 24 squares.

LIGHT LEMON SQUARES

*If you like the taste of lemon, you'll love these squares. This recipe comes from our Grandma Golde's cookbook, **Golde's Homemade Cookies**.*

HERE'S WHAT YOU NEED:

1 cup flour

¹/₂ cup (1 stick) of margarine

¹/₃ cup confectioners' sugar

Topping:

2 eggs

1 cup sugar

¹/₂ tablespoon flour

3 tablespoons lemon juice

HERE'S WHAT YOU DO:

1 Preheat oven to 350°.

2 In a medium bowl, mix the pastry ingredients together.

3 Press into a greased 8" x 8" pan.

4 Bake at 350° for 20 minutes.

5 Combine all of the topping ingredients together and beat until well-blended. Pour over baked pastry.

6 Return to oven. Bake an additional 20 to 25 minutes. Cool pan on wire rack before cutting.

7 Sprinkle with additional sifted confectioners' sugar.

Makes about 20 squares.

Special Occasions
Tea for Two

Want to do something very special for one of your grandparents or an older friend or neighbor? Invite that special person over for a pot of tea and cookies . . . . or, if he or she is housebound and can't get to your house, pack up a tea-party-in-a-basket, and make someone very happy.

HERE'S WHAT YOU NEED:

A small, pretty tablecloth or placemat
A flower or some pretty leaves in a vase or glass
A teapot, if you have one (not necessary)
Two cups and saucers
Cloth napkins, if you have them
2 teaspoons
3 tea bags
Slices of lemon
Honey or sugar
A little milk or cream
Some special cookies you just baked — like *Light Lemon Squares.*

HERE'S WHAT YOU DO:

1. Set up your tea table wherever you are — it can be on a table, on the floor, wherever will work for your special guest.
2. Put some water on to boil. Meanwhile, set out the cookies and napkins, the milk, lemon, and sugar or honey.
3. Place a tea bag in each cup or all the tea bags in the teapot and pour the boiling water over the bags. Let the bags set in the water (steep) about 2 minutes, then remove.
4. Serve the tea, and let your guest flavor it the way he or she likes. Pass the cookies.

P.S. If you don't know what to talk about, ask older people about what school was like when they were young and they will gladly tell you. Listen carefully, and ask a few questions. You will both have a wonderful time.

OATMEAL RAISIN COOKIES

Here's another of Grandma Golde's cookie recipes. You'll be surprised at how easy these delicious cookies are to bake.

HERE'S WHAT YOU NEED:

1½ cups rolled oats, uncooked
½ cup sugar
½ cup margarine, melted
1 egg, beaten
¾ cup flour
2 teaspoons baking powder
¼ teaspoon salt
5 teaspoons milk or water
1½ teaspoons vanilla extract
¾ cup seedless raisins
¼ cup nuts, chopped (optional)

HERE'S WHAT YOU DO:

1 Preheat the oven to 400°.

2 In a large bowl, combine the rolled oats and sugar.

3 Add the melted margarine and egg. Mix until well blended. Set aside.

4 Sift the flour, baking powder, and salt together. Add to the oat mixture and blend well. Mix in the milk, vanilla, raisins, and nuts.

5 Drop by rounded teaspoonfuls on a greased cookie sheet. Press down each spoonful with the back of a wet spoon or fork.

6 Bake at 400° for 10 minutes, until lightly browned. Transfer to a wire rack to cool.

Makes about 36 cookies.

JEWEL'S COOKIES

Our Grandma Golde started baking these with us when we were just little kids. Now she bakes them with our little cousins. They are always delicious!

HERE'S WHAT YOU NEED:

Pastry:

2 cups flour

2 sticks margarine, softened

1/2 cup sugar

2 egg yolks (See "How to Separate an Egg", page 130)

Filling:

1 jar of jam or preserves

Or maraschino cherries

Or Hershey's Chocolate Kisses™

HERE'S WHAT YOU DO:

1 Preheat oven to 350°.

2 Mix all of the pastry ingredients together.

3 Lightly grease a cookie sheet. Break off walnut-sized pieces of dough and roll them into balls. Flatten each ball in its center with your thumb and fill with whatever filling you choose.

4 Bake at 350° on lightly greased cookie sheet for 25 minutes. Cool on wire rack.

Makes about 36 cookies.

NO-BAKE CHOCOLATE CRUNCHIES

This is an easy cookie, and nobody ever knows what makes them so crunchy. You can vary the flavor by making these with peppermint chips or butterscotch chips, or just about any flavor you wish to try.

HERE'S WHAT YOU NEED:

1 package (8 ounces) chocolate chips, or other flavor

1 1/2 cups shredded coconut

1 cup chow mein noodles, slightly crushed

HERE'S WHAT YOU DO:

1 Melt the chocolate chips. Mix all of the ingredients together, being careful not to crush the noodles too much.

2 Line a cookie sheet with waxed paper. Drop cookie batter by teaspoonfuls. Refrigerate before serving.

Makes 24 drop cookies.

HOMEMADE PEANUT BUTTER CUP BARS

These taste almost as good as the storebought peanut butter cups and they are very easy to make.

HERE'S WHAT YOU NEED:

2 sticks margarine, melted

1½ cups graham cracker crumbs (about 10 to 11 crackers)

1 cup peanut butter

2 cups confectioners' sugar

1 large package (11 ounces) of chocolate chips or an 11-ounce chocolate bar

HERE'S WHAT YOU DO:

1 Mix the melted margarine, graham crackers, peanut butter, and confectioners' sugar together.

2 Pat into a 9" x 13" pan.

3 Melt the chocolate in the microwave or in the top of a double boiler (see this page). Spread melted chocolate over crumb mixture.

4 Refrigerate and cut into squares.

Makes 32 squares

Option: You can make these in small muffin cups instead, placing the crumb mixture on the bottom of each cup and then topping with the chocolate.

CLASSY COOKS

Double Boilers. If you don't have a microwave, melt the chocolate in a *double boiler*, but get some help from an adult. A double boiler is a small saucepan placed in a larger saucepan. Fill the large saucepan with a few inches of water and bring to a boil. Place the chocolate in the small saucepan, and put over the boiling water. The heat from the boiling water will melt the chocolate without burning it. Please get help from an adult when using a double boiler because handling two pans of very hot liquids at once can be double trouble!

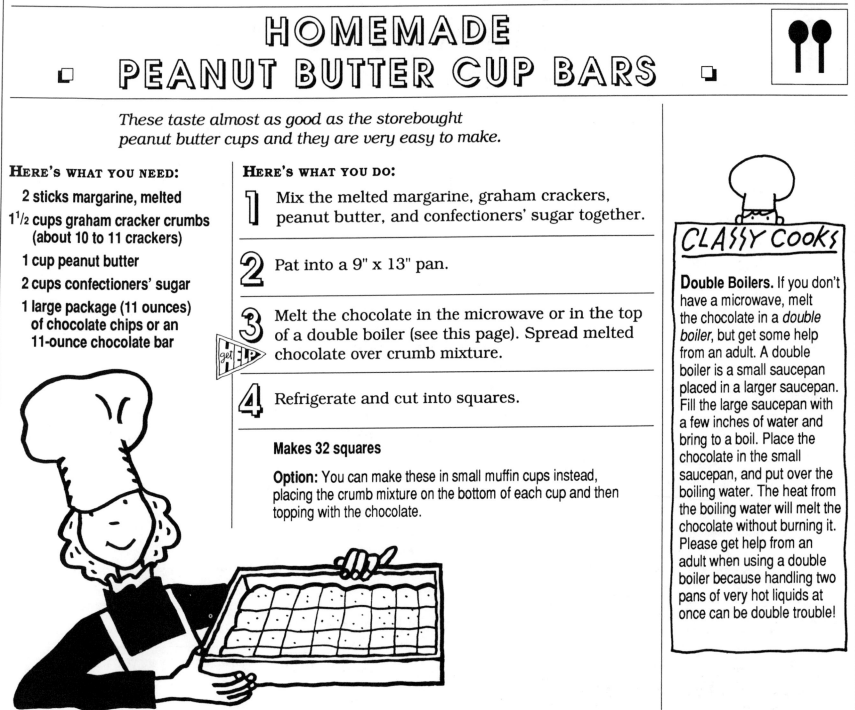

BANANA BOATS

Here is a special campfire treat whether you are camping at a famous campground or in your own backyard.

HERE'S WHAT YOU NEED:

Banana

Chocolate candy bar

Marshmallows, miniature or regular

Aluminum foil

HERE'S WHAT YOU DO:

1 Slice 1 banana lengthwise, not cutting all the way through.

2 Arrange bits of marshmallow and chocolate inside the sliced banana.

3 Wrap the entire banana in foil and place directly in the coals.

4 Cook until chocolate and marshmallow are melted, about 5 minutes or more depending on how hot your fire is.

Each banana makes enough for 1 person.

S'MORES

These have always been a delicious treat around a campfire.

HERE'S WHAT YOU NEED:

Graham crackers

Chocolate candy bars

Marshmallows

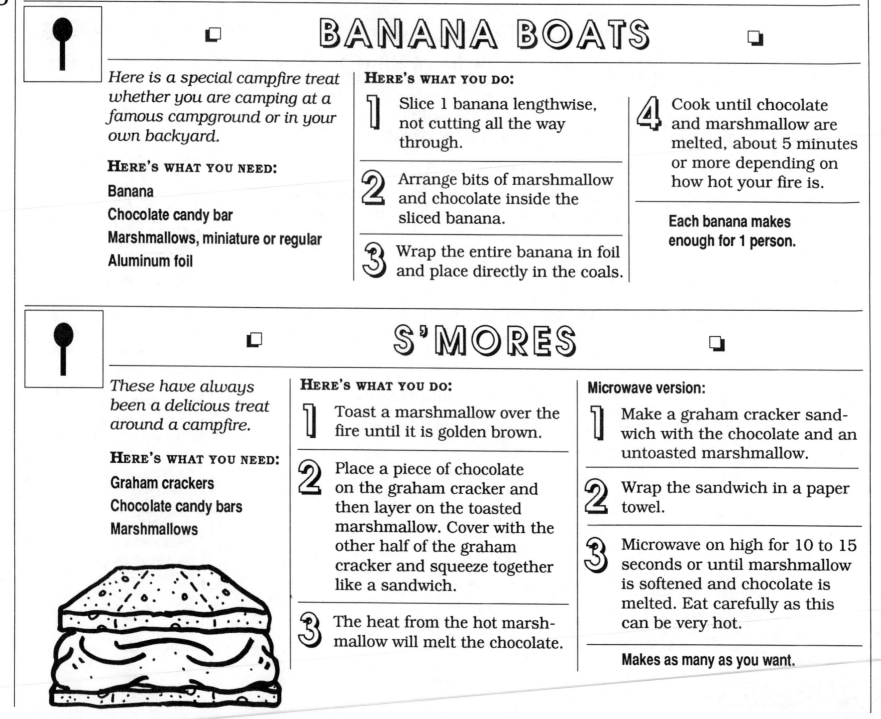

HERE'S WHAT YOU DO:

1 Toast a marshmallow over the fire until it is golden brown.

2 Place a piece of chocolate on the graham cracker and then layer on the toasted marshmallow. Cover with the other half of the graham cracker and squeeze together like a sandwich.

3 The heat from the hot marshmallow will melt the chocolate.

Microwave version:

1 Make a graham cracker sandwich with the chocolate and an untoasted marshmallow.

2 Wrap the sandwich in a paper towel.

3 Microwave on high for 10 to 15 seconds or until marshmallow is softened and chocolate is melted. Eat carefully as this can be very hot.

Makes as many as you want.

LAYERED CHOCOLATE CAKE

This is a great recipe. Even though there are a lot of ingredients, it is not difficult to make. Be sure to let your cake cool completely before frosting.

HERE'S WHAT YOU NEED:

- 2 cups cake flour, sifted
- 2 teaspoons baking powder
- $\frac{1}{2}$ teaspoon baking soda
- $\frac{1}{4}$ teaspoon salt
- $\frac{1}{2}$ cup plus 2 tablespoons cocoa
- $1\frac{1}{2}$ cups granulated sugar
- $\frac{1}{2}$ cup plus 2 tablespoons shortening (margarine or Crisco™)
- $\frac{1}{2}$ cup warm water
- $\frac{2}{3}$ cup milk
- 2 eggs
- 1 teaspoon vanilla extract

HERE'S WHAT YOU DO:

1. Preheat oven to 350°.

2. Sift together the flour, baking powder, baking soda, salt, cocoa, and sugar.

3. Add the shortening, water, milk, eggs, and vanilla extract. Blend with mixer on very low speed until the ingredients are thoroughly mixed and moistened.

4. Mix on medium speed for 3 minutes.

5. Pour the mixture into two 9"-layer cake pans that have been greased. Bake at 350° for 25 to 30 minutes or until the cake bounces back after being gently pressed in the center.

6. Cool in the pans on a wire rack 10 minutes before removing from the pans.

7. Let cool completely before frosting. See our *Chocolate Frosting* on page 149 or our *Creamy Vanilla Frosting* on page 150.

Makes enough for 12 people.

GRANDMA GOLDE'S FAMOUS CHEESE PIE

Every year, Sarah asks our Aunt Debby to make this for Thanksgiving. Of all the pies at our Thanksgiving dinner, this is the most popular one.

HERE'S WHAT YOU NEED:

Crust:

1¼ cups graham cracker crumbs

4 tablespoons margarine, melted

¼ cup sugar, or less according to taste

Filling:

2 eggs

¾ cup sugar

1 pound cream cheese

1 teaspoon vanilla extract

Topping:

1 cup sour cream

1 teaspoon vanilla extract

2 tablespoons sugar

HERE'S WHAT YOU DO:

1 Preheat oven to 350°.

2 To prepare the crust, mix the graham cracker crumbs, sugar, and the melted margarine together. Press into a greased 9" or 10" pie dish. Bake for 5 minutes, then remove from oven.

3 Beat the eggs, sugar, cream cheese, and vanilla together with a mixer. Beat for about 5 minutes.

4 Pour into pie crust and bake at 350° for 20 minutes.

5 While the pie is baking, mix the topping ingredients together in a small bowl.

6 After the pie bakes for the 20 minutes, remove it from the oven and pour on the topping. Spread it gently towards the sides so it covers the whole top. Turn oven up to 475° (this is very hot so have an adult help you) and bake for 5 minutes.

7 Remove pie from oven and let it cool. Then refrigerate until serving.

Makes at least 10 servings.

BIRTHDAY CUPCAKES

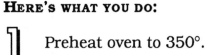

These are perfect for just about any occasion, but they are a lot of fun to prepare for birthdays or with a group of children if you are baby-sitting.

HERE'S WHAT YOU NEED:

2 cups flour

1½ cups sugar

½ cup shortening (margarine or Crisco™)

1 cup milk

3½ teaspoons baking powder

1 teaspoon salt

1 teaspoon vanilla extract

3 eggs

HERE'S WHAT YOU DO:

1 Preheat oven to 350°.

2 In a large bowl, combine all of the ingredients. Beat for 3 minutes, scraping the sides of the bowl with a rubber spatula often.

3 Line a cupcake pan with paper liners or grease well.

4 Pour in the batter (or use a soup ladle), filling each cup about half full.

5 Bake at 350° for 20 minutes. Cool completely before frosting with either *Chocolate Frosting* (see below), *Creamy Vanilla Frosting*, or *Cream Cheese Frosting*. Decorate with colorful sprinkles.

Makes 12 cupcakes.

Option: It is sometimes fun to put a surprise in these cupcakes. After you have poured the batter into the cups, poke a jelly bean, a Hershey's Chocolate Kiss™, a half teaspoon of jam, a couple of chocolate chips, or raisins into the batter for a delicious surprise.

CHOCOLATE FROSTING

Although many frostings seem difficult to apply smoothly, this one is surprisingly easy to work with and tastes delicious, too.

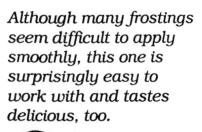

HERE'S WHAT YOU NEED:

⅓ cup butter, softened

2 squares (1 ounce each) unsweetened chocolate, melted and cooled

2 cups confectioners' sugar

1½ teaspoons vanilla extract

About 2 tablespoons milk

HERE'S WHAT YOU DO:

1 Mix the butter and melted chocolate together.

2 Stir in the confectioners' sugar.

3 Beat in the vanilla and milk (a little at a time) until frosting is smooth, creamy, and of good spreading consistency (not too stiff, but not soupy either).

Makes enough for 1 cake or 12 cupcakes.

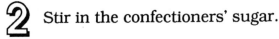

CREAM CHEESE FROSTING

This frosting goes very well with cakes that you want to decorate with some fruit or berries like **Fourth of July Cake***. It is also great on carrot cake or spice cake.*

HERE'S WHAT YOU NEED:

1 package (8 ounces) cream cheese, at room temperature

1 box confectioners' sugar

1 teaspoon vanilla extract

12 tablespoons butter, at room temperature

HERE'S WHAT YOU DO:

1 Place in a bowl and cream all ingredients together. If frosting is too stiff, add some milk or cream, 1 teaspoon at a time.

Makes enough for 1 cake or 12 cupcakes.

CREAMY VANILLA FROSTING

You can add food coloring to make it the color you want, but only add a drop or two at a time.

HERE'S WHAT YOU NEED:

3 cups confectioners' sugar

1/3 cup butter, softened

1 1/2 teaspoons vanilla extract

About 2 tablespoons milk

HERE'S WHAT YOU DO:

1 Mix confectioners' sugar and butter together.

2 Stir in vanilla and milk.

3 Beat until smooth and creamy.

4 Frosts a 9" x 13" sheet cake or two 8" or 9" layered cakes. (Be sure to always frost the top of each layer so you won't have as many crumbs to bother with.)

Makes enough for 1 cake or 12 cupcakes.

RAINBOW JELLO™

This recipe takes a while, but it's definitely worth the effort (it looks great). We have a lot of fun making this. You can vary the colors by choosing different flavors. Also, you can add a little Cool Whip® once the gelatin is cool, but not yet set, to half of each flavor (split into separate bowls). This will give you more contrast between the layers.

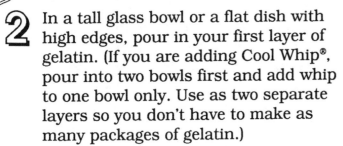

HERE'S WHAT YOU NEED:

1 package (3 ounces) **apricot or orange gelatin**

1 package (3 ounces) **lemon or lime gelatin**

1 package (3 ounces) **cherry or strawberry gelatin**

HERE'S WHAT YOU DO:

1 Prepare one package of gelatin according to package directions.

2 In a tall glass bowl or a flat dish with high edges, pour in your first layer of gelatin. (If you are adding Cool Whip®, pour into two bowls first and add whip to one bowl only. Use as two separate layers so you don't have to make as many packages of gelatin.)

3 Set in the refrigerator until gelatin has set firmly.

4 Prepare another package of gelatin. Set it in the refrigerator until almost firm, and then pour onto base layer. (It is a good idea to use a ladle to prevent breaking the surface of the other layer.)

5 Keep doing these steps until each package of gelatin has been used. Look at the side of the dish and you should see a rainbow of color.

6 Before serving, top with our *Homemade Whipped Cream* (see page 97).

Makes as many servings as you want.

BAKED APPLES WITH BUTTERSCOTCH SAUCE

You probably know how good caramel apples are. Well, these are even better — plus they don't get stuck in your teeth!

HERE'S WHAT YOU NEED:

Large cooking apples, 1 for each person
Brown sugar
Cinnamon
Margarine

Butterscotch Sauce (for 6 apples):
$\frac{1}{2}$ cup milk
 1 tablespoon flour
 1 egg
$\frac{1}{2}$ cup brown sugar
Pinch salt
$\frac{1}{2}$ teaspoon margarine
$\frac{1}{2}$ teaspoon vanilla extract

HERE'S WHAT YOU DO:

1 Preheat oven to 375°. Wash and core apples. Peel a little skin from just around the top. Place in a baking dish.

2 Fill the center of each apple with some brown sugar. Sprinkle on some cinnamon and dot with about 1 teaspoon margarine for each apple.

3 Pour some water in the bottom of the pan and cover with aluminum foil. Bake at 375° for 40 to 60 minutes or until tender but not broken or mushy.

4 Meanwhile, to make the sauce, put all the ingredients in a medium-sized saucepan and mix well. Boil over medium heat until quite thick.

get HELP

5 When apples are ready, place each apple on a serving dish (be careful of the steam when you lift off the foil). Have someone help you ladle the hot butterscotch sauce over the apples and top with some whipped cream if you like.

Make as many as you want.

Options: These apples are also delicious without the butterscotch sauce. You can serve them plain, with a little whipped cream, some honey dribbled down the sides, or some hot maple syrup.

MORE GOOD BOOKS FROM

WILLIAMSON PUBLISHING

To order additional copies of **Kids Cook!**, please enclose $12.95 per copy plus $2.50 shipping and handling. Follow "To Order" instructions on the last page. Thank you.

THE KIDS' NATURE BOOK
365 Indoor/Outdoor Activities and Experiences
by Susan Milord

Winner of the Parents' Choice Gold Award for learning and doing books, *The Kids' Nature Book* is loved by children, grandparents, and friends alike. Simple projects and activities emphasize fun while quietly reinforcing the wonder of the world we all share. Packed with facts and fun!

160 pages, 11 x 8½, 425 illustrations
Quality paperback, $12.95

KIDS CREATE!
Art & Craft Experiences for 3- to 9-year-olds
by Laurie Carlson

What's the most important experience for children ages 3 to 9? Why to create something by themselves. Carlson provides over 150 creative experiences ranging from making dinosaur sculptures to clay cactus gardens, from butterfly puppets to windsocks. Plenty of help for the parents working with the kids, too! A delightfully innovative book.

160 pages, 11 x 8½, over 400 illustrations,
Quality paperback, $12.95

KIDS & WEEKENDS
Creative Ways to Make Special Days
by Avery Hart and Paul Mantell

Packed with truly creative ways to play, have fun, learn, grow, and build self-esteem and positive relationships, this book is a must for every child. Hart and Mantell will inspire us all to transform some part of every weekend — even if it is only 30 minutes — into a special experience. Everything from backyard nature to putting on a magic show to creating a bird sanctuary to writing a book about yourself to environmentally sound activities, indoors and out. Whatever your interests, no matter how busy you are, kids and their families will savor these special weekend moments.

176 pages, 11 x 8½, over 400 illustrations,
Quality paperback, $12.95

ADVENTURES IN ART
Art & Craft Experiences for 7- to 14-year-olds
by Susan Milord

Imagine an art book that encourages children to explore, to experience, to touch and to see, to learn and to create . . . imagine a true adventure in art. Here's a book that teaches artisan's skills without stifling creativity. Covers making handmade papers, puppets, masks, paper seascapes, seed art, tin can lantern, berry ink, still life, silk screen, batiking, carving and so much more. Perfect for the older child. Let the adventure begin!

160 pages, 11 x 8½, 500 illustrations
Quality paperback, $12.95

KIDS LEARN AMERICA!
Bringing Geography to Life With People, Places, and History
by Patricia Gordon and Reed C. Snow

Over 44 million Americans can't find the Pacific Ocean on a map. Let Gordon and Snow challenge your kids to know where they are and where they're going with this all-new approach encompassing the human-earth connection. This book breathes life into geography with experiential, hands-on learning. Kids of all ages will enjoy the 52 state challenges, games, memory techniques, trivia, and most of all, knowing where they fit into this great expansive country.

176 pages, 11 x 8½, over 500 maps and illustrations,
Quality paperback, $12.95

DOING CHILDREN'S MUSEUMS
A Guide to 250 Hands-On Museums
by Joanne Cleaver

Turn an ordinary day into a spontaneous "vacation" by taking a child to some of the 250 participatory children's museums, discovery rooms, and nature centers covered in this highly acclaimed, one-of-a-kind book. Filled with museum specifics to help you pick and plan the perfect place for the perfect day, Cleaver has created a most valuable resource for anyone who loves kids! Newly revised!

270 pages, 6 x 9,
Quality paperback, $13.95

PARENTS ARE TEACHERS, TOO
Enriching Your Child's First Six Years
by Claudia Jones

Be the best teacher your child ever has. Jones shares hundreds of ways to help any child learn in playful home situations. Lots on developing reading, writing, math skills. Plenty on creative and critical thinking, too. A book you'll love using!

192 pages, 6 x 9, illustrations,
Quality paperback, $9.95

MORE PARENTS ARE TEACHERS, TOO
Encouraging Your 6- to 12-Year-Old
by Claudia Jones

Help your children be the best they can be! When parents are involved, kids do better. When kids do better, they feel better, too. Here's a wonderfully creative book of ideas, activities, teaching methods and more to help you help your children over the rough spots and share in their growing joy in achieving. Plenty on reading, writing, math, problem-solving, creative thinking. Everything for parents who want to help but not push their children.

226 pages, 6 x 9, illustrations,
Quality paperback, $10.95

THE HOMEWORK SOLUTION
by Linda Agler Sonna

Put homework responsibilities where they belong — in the student's lap! Here it is! The simple remedy for the millions of parents who are tired of waging the never-ending nightly battle over kids' homework. Dr. Sonna's "One Step Solution" will relieve parents, kids, and their siblings of the ongoing problem within a single month.

192 pages, 6 x 9,
Quality paperback, $10.95

THE BROWN BAG COOKBOOK
Nutritious Portable Lunches for Kids and Grown-Ups
by Sara Sloan

Here are more than 1,000 brown bag lunch ideas with 150 recipes for simple, quick, nutritious lunches that kids will love. Breakfast ideas, too! This popular book is now in its ninth printing as more and more people realize how important every meal is to our health!

192 pages, 8¼ x 7¼, illustrations,
Quality paperback, $9.95

GOLDE'S HOMEMADE COOKIES
by Golde Soloway

Over 50,000 copies of this marvelous cookbook have been sold. Now it's in its second edition with 135 of the most delicious cookie recipes imaginable. *Publishers Weekly* says, "Cookies are her chosen realm and how sweet a world it is to visit." You're sure to agree!

162 pages, 8¼ x 7¼ , illustrations,
Quality paperback, $8.95

CARING FOR OLDER CATS & DOGS
Extending Your Pet's Healthy Life
by Robert Anderson, DVM and Barbara J. Wrede

Here's the only book that will help you distinguish the signs of natural aging from pain and suffering, that will help you care for your pet with compassion and knowledge. How to help your older pet, how to nourish, nurture, and nurse your cat or dog, and finally when and how to let go. Medically sound with reasonable homeopathic remedies, too, mixed with practical advice and compassion. Every older pet deserves an owner who has read this!

192 pages, 6 x 9, illustrations,
Quality paperback, $10.95

Easy-to-Make STUFFED ANIMALS & ALL THE TRIMMINGS
by Jodie Davis

Bunnies, dinosaurs, piglets, a friendly cow, kittens, fawns — these are just a few of the wonderful, cuddly stuffed animals you can make with Jodie Davis' step-by-step instructions, plus patterns for clothes to dress these precious creatures in.

208 pages, 8½ x 11, 150 illustrations and patterns,
Quality paperback, $13.95

Easy-to-Make TEDDY BEARS & ALL THE TRIMMINGS
by Jodie Davis

Now you can make the most lovable, huggable, plain or fancy teddy bears imaginable, for a fraction of store-bought costs. Step-by-step instructions and easy patterns drawn to actual size for large, soft-bodied bears, quilted bears, and even jointed bears. Plus patterns for clothes, accessories — even teddy bear furniture!

192 pages, 8½ x 11, illustrations and patterns,
Quality paperback, $13.95

SUGAR-FREE TODDLERS
by Susan Watson

Here are over 100 recipes for nutrition-filled breakfasts, lunches, snacks, beverages, and more. And best of all, they're all sugar-free. Plus ratings for hundreds of store-bought products, too. If you have young children, they need you to have this book.

160 pages, 8¼ x 7¼, 150 illustrations,
Quality paperback, $9.95

To Order:

At your bookstore or order directly from Williamson Publishing. We accept Visa and MasterCard (please include number and expiration date), or send check to:

Williamson Publishing Company
Church Hill Road, P.O. Box 185
Charlotte, Vermont 05445

Toll-free phone orders with credit cards:
1-800-234-8791

Please add $2.50 for postage and handling. Satisfaction is guaranteed or full refund without questions or quibbles.